Adult Religious Education
Theory to Practice

Adult Religious Education
Theory to Practice

by Gemma Brennan
and Kevin Cronin

Illustrations by HARO

With a foreword by
Bishop David Konstant
and a postscript by
Tony McCaffry

MAYHEW McCRIMMON
Great Wakering Essex England

First published in Great Britain in 1984 by
MAYHEW McCRIMMON LTD
Great Wakering   Essex   England

© 1984 Mayhew McCrimmon Ltd

ISBN 0 85597 364 1

Cover Design: Nick Snode
Typesetting: Phoenix Typesetters Ltd, Southend-on-Sea, Essex

Printed by Bemrose Printing Ltd, Derby, England

Contents

Foreword

WE NOW take it for granted that growing in faith, and everything that assists this growth, is a lifelong process. Recent church statements on education have all made the same point, that religious education for the adult is never complete. In a report to the Bishops' Conference of England and Wales on the Educative Task of the Catholic Community we read (*Signposts and Homecomings*, p143): 'Foremost among our immediate practical conclusions is the absolute centrality of sustained adult Christian education. The life of the individual Catholic and the health of the whole Church alike demand commitment to this as the single most important educational activity of the Church. Every other educational initiative in the Church depends on an effective approach to this work. Nothing can excuse its omission or neglect.' This strong statement echoes, for example, what was said in *The General Catechetical Directory* (Rome, 1971; paras 19, 20, 92 ff) and in *The Easter People* (the bishops' response to the National Pastoral Congress, 1980; paras 145 ff).

It is essential that we move from words to action, and from theory to practice. Moreover it is necessary that we put our ambition for adult religious education into practice at the local level — as local as possible. Plans for developing this work and co-ordinating it nationally must of course go ahead, but these are likely to succeed only insofar as there are strongly developed local initiatives in different parts of the country.

Sister Gemma Brennan and Father Kevin Cronin have done pioneering work in adult RE in one large diocese over more than a decade. This handbook has been written as part of the fruit of their experience. It is enormously welcome. It has just the sort of practical slant to it that will help those involved in the adult religious education scene move from theory to practice.

My hope is that just as about a century and a half ago we began as a Church to put into practice ideas about the education of children in the faith, so now we will begin to make real the hopes of Church in regard to the continuing education in faith of our adult members. I am delighted to recommend this book and to welcome it as an important contribution to the adult religious education scene.

+ David Konstant

Bishop David Konstant
Chairman,
Department of Christian Doctrine and Formation

Introduction

THIS BOOK is written for the ever increasing number of people who are interested in adult religious education. More especially it is written for those who, like ourselves, may be involved in enabling adults to plan and to operate this service — who prefer to work with adults rather than just for them.

In writing the book we have been helped, guided and encouraged by the members of the Adult Education Committee of the diocese of Westminster, individually and collectively; by Pat Collins, the chairman, Martin O'Connor, Joan Adams, Susan Bano, the Rev Desmond Beirne, CM, Janice Burn, the Rev Gerry Burke, the Rev James Crampsie, SJ, Nora Foley, Imelda Gardiner, Sister Margaret Leckenby, SCJA, Patrick Lynn, the Rev Kevin Moran, Mary Smith, the Rev Richard Wakeling, Kathie Walsh, Canon Harold Winstone, Alan Whelan and Sister Gilberte Regnard, IBVM, secretary.

We record our special indebtedness to Gerard Egan and Michael Cowan and their publishers for permission to quote extensively in Part Two of the book from their work *People in Systems;* and also to Father Justin Arbery-Price, OSB, of Ampleforth College, for assisting us in our use of the Egan/Cowan planning model. For the illustrations we are grateful to Haro Hodson, whose drawings in the *Daily Mail* are familiar to millions.

The book concludes with a postscript from Tony McCaffry, the present Principal of the Westminster Adult Religious Education Centre.

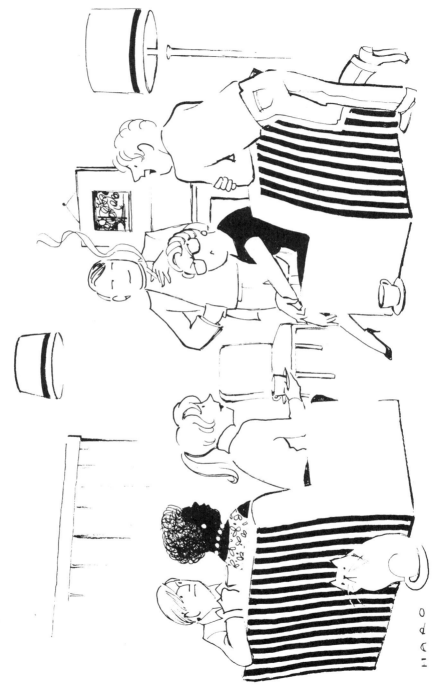

'There should be a visible decision to make adult Christian education the priority.'

PART ONE

Lifelong religious education – the adult stage

WHEN on Wednesday, June 2nd, 1982, Pope John Paul II addressed the assembled Catholics at Pontcomna Fields, Cardiff, on the last day of his historic visit to Britain, he had a special message for each of the groups assembled to hear him. To 'these little ones who are about to receive Holy Communion for the first time'[1] he spoke of Jesus who was coming to them in a new way. To their parents he said: 'Your love for Christ has made this day possible. You are your children's first teachers in the ways of faith ... show them the truths of our faith and the values of the Gospel.'[2] To their teachers he said: 'You are heirs of a great tradition, and the People of God are in your debt.' Finally, he had a word for the priests who were present, and he must have had a special reason for the particular charge he now gave them. 'Beloved brother priests ... I know that your bishops are anxious to develop throughout England and Wales practical programmes of adult religious education in the faith. I urge you to be in the vanguard of those efforts, which are so important for the vitality of the Church.'[3]

This book could have been written as a handbook for those anxious to implement the papal injunction.

Adult religious education! Is there any special need for it today? Is it any more needed today than it was in the time of our grandparents? And does anyone want it?

The delegates who attended the National Pastoral Congress held in Liverpool in 1980 — and they came, it should be noted, from every diocese and practically every parish in England and Wales — certainly considered that it was needed and wanted. Among the requests submitted by the Congress to the Hierarchy, one was for 'a positive visible decision to make adult Christian education the priority, accepting the resource implications of this.'[4] The

Hierarchy's response to this in the *Easter People* document in the autumn of the same year was an unqualified acceptance.

> 'The continuing Christian education and formation of adult members of the Church must become a priority in our church's educational labours. Any genuine renewal of the life and work of the Church will in the end largely depend upon commitment to this work. The precise way forward is not yet plain, but it is obvious we walk in this direction. We willingly accept the practical implications of this decision, including the allocation of personnel and resources that may be proved necessary.'[5]

What has caused this sudden interest in the furthering of the religious education of adults? Von Hugel, writing at the turn of the century, could explain what is now the situation. In a wonderfully simple but as yet unsurpassed analysis of religious development, which to him was not separable from human development, he saw but three stages in the process. He called childhood the institutional stage, adolescence the critical stage and adulthood the mystical stage.[6]

Von Hugel envisaged the unreflecting, receptive attitude of the child giving way in time to the critical analytical approach of the adolescent. The Creed received and accepted in childhood is subjected to scrutiny and even possible rejection. Without this stage there could never be progress to the third stage, personal adult commitment. The faith would remain at the stage of childhood, an acceptance because someone in authority has said so.

In the grip of a bad tradition, culturally speaking, most Catholics over the last hundred years remained at the childhood stage — loyal, obedient children before a wise omniscient authority. The consequence was a split between religion and life, and a voiceless passivity.

Now there is an awakening! At the Liverpool Congress it was evident that an adult community had reached Von Hugel's second 'critical' stage.

The Liverpool Congress resolution and the Pope's subsequent appeal to the clergy at Cardiff are sufficient evidence, if evidence is needed, that a great deal is happening in the field of adult religious education. In every diocese in the country qualified persons, laymen and laywomen as well as priests and religious, are being recruited or are being prepared to work in this field. Many interesting projects are being planned and attempted. The movement is gaining momentum.

A recently published examination of the working of adult education in a London borough carried the very telling title *The Poor Cousin*.[7] The title indicated the author's opinion of the Inner London Education Authority's level of concern and investment in adult education.

Up to the Liverpool Pastoral Congress of 1980 it could truly be said to the ecclesiastical authorities of England and Wales that religious education was still very much the 'poor cousin' in terms of funding, resources and pastoral strategy and general interest. Now, quite unexpectedly and much to his surprise, our poor cousin finds himself riding what has all the appearance of a modest band-wagon.

Removing a misconception

Before we proceed any further, before we examine the various attempts to provide a service of adult religious education to those who have asked for it, it is important to remove a misconception about the nature and the scope of religious education.

Religious education is concerned directly with beliefs, and this is not quite the same thing as faith. The recitation of the Creed is, strange as it may seem, not of its nature an act of faith but a statement of beliefs. I believe *in* ...

I believe God — *that* is an act of faith; it is relational. Beliefs are consequent. Most Christians share the same faith. They differ in their beliefs, and their elaboration into doctrines and moral precepts.

When we speak of adult religious education and formation, it is of beliefs and their implication that we are speaking. Deepening of personal faith is the intention, but it is not an automatic consequence. Faith is God's gift: it is personal; it is the life hidden with Christ in God. It cannot be measured.

Since the First Ecumenical Council held in Jerusalem in AD49 there has been development in doctrine, that is of beliefs, as every theologian from Augustine to Newman has told us. This is, properly speaking, the field of adult religious education. Until recently, due to a loose identification of faith with beliefs, we have failed as a church to introduce our people even to the concept of development. As a result, people are disturbed at the very hint of change.

To Newman, change was of the essence. 'To live is to change. To be perfect is to have changed often.' Have the beliefs of the Church changed all that much in our time? Of course there are some elements of the Church's belief and teaching that have changed little or not at all; but one should not miss the point that in the last two decades, leading up to and stored in the documents of the Second Vatican Council, there has been the most colossal re-think and restatement of Christian beliefs of the entire 2,000 years of the Church's history.

The attitude of the Church to the world in which we live, to people of other beliefs or of none, to the nature and mission of its founder, to its own nature, its mission, its working, its involvement in and with and for the world — in all this there has been such re-thinking that the shock waves are with us still.

This is what adult religious education is all about.

Motivation — the prerequisite to adult education

A key statement in the Vatican Council document *Church in the Modern World* is that the separation of religion from life is among the worst evils of our time. The fact that religion is seen in general as separate from, over against, above or in addition to life, clearly minimises the relevance of any attempt at adult religious education and formation for the average Catholic. For the adult Christian, if there is little or no relevance there is little or no motivation.

The acceptance of the two-world view, with the resulting division into secular and sacred, has caused people to live as if there were no connection between one and the other. What was said in church seemed to have little relevance to real life. Revelation was presented in terms of the deposit of faith, spiritual life, life of the soul, after life. It was not thought of as present and active in man's day-to-day experience. But God's revelation is not a religious veneer on things, nor a religious message to be injected into people. It is the recognition of God already active in our lives.[8]

In addition there was the inbuilt passivity of the laity in face of an infallible authority. Over the recent centuries the faithful have been conditioned to a one-way teaching method which gave no opportunity for exchange of any kind. This was detrimental to priests and people. The people had little or no way of questioning or appraising the religious truth presented to them in the Sunday sermon, the Mass liturgy, in devotional exercises, in parish missions or retreats. It is true that among the laity themselves there was plenty of appraisal and also more or less good humoured criticism. But on the whole passive acceptance of beliefs spelt out in school was continued into adult life.

The search for meaning is common to all adults, whatever their religion or none, as they live out and reflect upon their experience. All adults give some sort of meaning to their lives: they have 'faith' in something, someone. Adult religious education must, in its attempt to bridge the gap between religion and life, help people to recognise, to identify what for them gives meaning, what is faith for them.[9]

This change of approach since the Second Vatican Council was given an immense boost in England and Wales by the Liverpool Pastoral Congress.[10] The clear statement of the importance of adult religious education and formation coming from the Congress demanded immediate action and reallocation of resources. At the Congress, the Church in England and Wales woke up to find its laity had come of age. This should have surprised nobody except those who still maintain the two-world view. A quick look at the world of industry, commerce and the professions sees these same adults involved in policy-making, consultation and decision-making with management and their fellow workers. Yet many of these people were reluctant to involve themselves in the church any more than by regular attendance at Mass and occasionally at the sacraments. It is not without significance that when the hierarchy appealed to the laity to increase their financial contribution to the Church, the response was negligible: they had no incentive to maintain a system in the operation of which they were not involved. Motivation was minimal.

Thomas Aquinas, writing seven centuries ago on the role of the educator, made the point that the person to be educated[11] is the primary agent in his/her own education. Unless he/she is active, self-activating, if he/she is merely submissive, then there is no real education. Thomas Aquinas did not use the word motivation; but everything he said spelt it out. The conclusion is that adults will undertake continuing adult religious education only if they can see in what is offered something they genuinely want.

NOTES

1. *The Pope Teaches,* CTS, 1982, p221.
2. op cit p221.

3. op cit p222.
4. Congress Report, Section E; Recommendation 1.
5. *Easter People,* p145.
6. *Mystical Element in Religion,* by S. Von Hugel (Bent, 1908).
7. *The Poor Cousin,* by Michael Newman (George Allen and Unwin, London, 1979).
8. cf *Love and Meaning in Religious Education,* by D. J. O'Leary and T. Sallnow, Oxford University Press, 1982, p5, for a fuller discussion.
9. James Fowler, in his book *Faith Development,* uses the word 'faith' in this broad sense.
10. Congress Report, cf p27, par 4.
11. *De Magistro - Summer Theologica.*

PART TWO

The planning process
A planning model

DURING the 1970s and 80s, as a result of the Second Vatican Council, two most interesting developments have been taking place in the Catholic community of England and Wales.

Firstly, many of the laity are looking to their parishes to provide them with opportunities to continue their religious education. They are increasingly conscious of the fact that their religious education ceased for all practical purposes when they left school.

Secondly, diocesan authorities, keenly aware of the importance and urgency of the matter, are everywhere setting up agencies to advise and assist. These agencies come in a variety of forms. A particular individual, or a group of individuals, is asked to assume responsibility for the work. A committee is formed to investigate the needs and to recommend action. Diocesan pastoral councils include members who have this as a special responsibility. A special diocesan centre is established to assist in the local communities who are working in the field. This is distinct from what was the catechetical centre for the schools.

The Hierarchy document *The Easter People* strongly recommends the setting up of adult religious education centres. 'These small beginnings of adult religious education and formation at parish level', it states[1], 'need support and guidance from the local diocese. We hope that wherever practical there can be set up an adequately staffed adult education centre whose task it will be to advise those working at the local level, to train leaders for this work and to plan more substantial courses than local organisers may be able to manage.'

In our view, a centre which operates in conjunction with a committee which is truly representative of the adult community, is a good arrangement. It is ideal if the officers of the centre are regarded as the executive arm of the committee and report regularly to it.

To illustrate the manner in which a diocesan service agency such as an adult education centre can be of assistance to a local community, consider the case of a parish which so far has not attempted to provide any adult religious education for its people, other than through the liturgy and through parish social life. Now, suddenly, it is asked for. The request may have come from a particular parishioner or group of parishioners; from a parish society or association; from the priest himself; or it may have come in response to an approach from the diocesan centre. The diocesan centre is invited in, to advise and assist. What can it do? What should it do?

What it definitely should *not* do is prescribe a definite course of action and proceed to organise and conduct it. The centre should be an enabling agency. Its function is to supplement the local initiative, not to supplant it; to help the local adults to decide on the particular educational activity that would suit their members, then to help them to plan it, and finally to achieve it.

This is not an easy thing to do. Adult religious education is an activity that takes many forms and ranges over a wide terrain. There is no master plan into which everything could be conveniently fitted. There are, however, some basic principles of organisation and management that could serve as guidelines: principles that are equally applicable in the case of a group planning a service of adult religious education for a parish and, say, a manufacturing firm devising and marketing a new product. The people and the system might be different but the principles determining action could be the same.

Egan and Cowan, in their book *People in Systems: a Model for Development in the Human Service Professions and Education,*[2] have devised a very useful and adaptable model for the guidance of those engaged in planning the type of service we are considering. We intend to use it as our planning model. Its essential elements are:

1. Those chosen to operate the system (in this case those planning an adult religious educational activity) should have the ability to know and to apply the principles of adult behaviour.
2. They should be able:
    — to assess the *needs* and *wants* of people;
    — to translate these into *general aims;*

— to develop these aims into *specific goals;*
— finally, to shape the goals into *projects,* making use of such *knowledge* and *skills* and *other resources* as are available.
3. They should recognise that:
— there should be *structure;*
— *relationships* should be clear;
— *communication* must be encouraged;
— a good *atmosphere* is important;
— account must be taken of the *environment.*

In the pages that follow we shall explain the elements of this model in more detail.

The planning group

THE FIRST requirement of the Egan/Cowan model is that those entrusted with the task of planning and organising a programme of adult religious education should have the ability to understand and apply what the authors term 'the principles of behaviour'. They should be selected because they are considered to be the right people for the job.

What are the criteria for selecting a planning group? Not just knowledge of the faith and commitment to it, but an awareness of the principles of human behaviour. This may sound very daunting; but if the group is going to be responsible for adult religious education, then it must have the authority for doing it. This authority is not simply the blessing of the bishop or the parish council, but more importantly the power to do the task. This power lies largely in the necessary skills, together with a true vision of what the religious education of the adult entails in our contemporary Christian society.

Christianity, 'the faith', to use the accepted phrase, has to do with life. One of the most compelling assertions of the Second Vatican Council was that the divorce of religion from life is the great evil of our day. Human life is the agenda of faith. To grow, to develop in the faith, is to become more human, and this development is indissolubly tied to personal development, to interpersonal relationships at all levels, to relationship with God. The Gospel, the Good News, is about salvation in Jesus from all in our selves, in our relationships with others, that prevents us as individuals, communities, nations, mankind itself, from becoming truly human.

Those who plan the religious education of their fellow adults must at least be aware of what helps and what hinders people, as individuals or as communities, including the Church itself, from growing in that kind of faith. Let us take a closer look at those 'principles of behaviour' that Egan/Cowan consider so important.

When adults achieve a measure of success, no matter how modest, they must be able to reward themselves, if only by the pleasure of having accomplished something successfully. But reward that is wrongly bestowed, as for instance to defer to the 'important' member of the group, even though what he/she says or does is wrong, is self-defeating. Rewarding or commending people for not doing something, or just avoiding trouble, is counter productive. It would be wrong, for instance, to embark on a study programme of social justice in a particular area and to ignore a blatant example of injustice in the area on the ground that it might give offence to some people.

The skills which are used and which are required in the learning situation — the skills of discussing, of summarising, even the skill of listening — should be suitably modelled for the benefit of those concerned. Seeing a skill demonstrated is not enough. It must also be practised; that is, there must be assessment and explicit training of participants. We readily recognise this when it comes to dancing, swimming, playing an instrument. It is even more true of inter-personal skills. In the case of the planners themselves, the skill of 'shaping', of proceeding step by step towards the realisation of a particular project, is again important. The planning group would have to organise their work in small enough steps so that they could get started, build momentum, and hit the hard parts only when they were ready for them.

So far we have discussed the qualities to be looked for in those entrusted with the task of planning an adult religious educational activity in a particular area. How are such people discovered? How are they brought together?

Let us return to the situation described in the previous section, which so far has not attempted to provide any such service for its adults and where a request for such a service has now been made. What should be done? First, the support of the parish council, if there is one, should be invoked. Many parishes nowadays have councils; and the constant complaint one hears is that they feel they have no power, or have nothing of significance to do. They feel they are involved in the 'maintenance' of the parish, not in its 'mission', though they might not use these words. Let the parish council, therefore, be the first to consider such an important matter as the setting up of adult religious education within the parish. If they like the idea, then the venture will have the advantage of starting with the official approval of the parish through its administrative body.

Here we make a strong plea for the parish at this stage to entrust the entire project to a specially formed planning group, who will be responsible for deciding which particular form of adult religious education to adopt, then for conducting and supervising the work until it is successfully concluded. It might be tempting — but the temptation should be resisted — to opt immediately for a particular type of activity and then to ask the parish clergy or the RE teachers in the school to plan and to conduct it. A group of parishioners, those with special interest in the work, with sufficient time to devote to it, would be much more likely to make a success of the enterprise.

Much care should be taken in the formation of the planning group. This is a very delicate matter. Not everyone who volunteers would necessarily be suitable. In some way a number of adults — five to eight — should be selected. Some parishes have a parish representative for adult religious education, some a religious education co-ordinator, others again a parish pastoral assistant. These should help with the selection. Ideally the members of the proposed new planning group should not be members of the parish council and should not hold any administrative post in the parish. Conflict of interests alone, and pressure on time, would only perpetuate the pattern which has existed for too long of the same people always being involved in everything.

The group should consist as far as possible of men and women of different ages, different backgrounds — industry, the professions, management — and different groups in adult religious education, e.g. parents. Include a member of the black community, if there is one, or of any sizeable immigrant group. One of the parish clergy would normally be included in the selection. The addition of one or two members of the diocesan adult religious education agency would complete the planning group. They would become an integral part of the group, removing the sense of *them* and *us,* while bringing to the group the benefit of their special skill and experience.

Here is a diagram of the Planning Group:

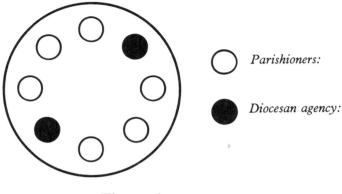

Figure 1

It is worth remarking that some parishes already plan adult religious education on an ecumenical basis: their planning groups include members from the different churches, sometimes from their diocesan or circuit or district adult education committees.

The parish is not, of course, the only body that might wish to provide a service of adult religious education for its members. A group of parishes — a deanery, let us say — is often better able to provide this than an individual parish. So, too, could be a primary or a secondary school with contacts in one or more parishes. A national organisation such as the Catholic Marriage Advisory Council, or a parish society such as the Catholic Women's League, might also wish to plan and conduct an adult education activity for members and for others. In all these instances there is need to begin by setting up a planning group on lines similar to those described. Once constituted and aware of its brief, its powers, the planning group can begin.

NOTES

1. *The Easter People,* par 152.
2. Brooks Cole Publishing Co, Monterey, California, USA, 1979.

Discover needs and wants

THE planning group are having their first session. They realise the problem facing them. They have to decide how to go about it.

The first step in the planning process, if they follow the Egan/Cowan model, is to consider the adult community for whom they hope to provide a service, and to be clear in their own minds what it is that these adults need and what it is they want. It is important that they should realise at the outset that 'needs' and 'wants' are not the same thing.

'I think I know what they want,' an informed parish priest or head teacher might say. 'They want a good series of instructions on the sacraments.' Just a minute! Could it be that the good priest or the good head teacher is confusing two things — what the people need and what they want? A boy needs a bath. He knows it; everyone knows it. But he doesn't want it. Does it make any difference? In the case of the boy, not one bit in the world. He will get the bath, and he knows he will. In the case of most adults, you cannot get them to accept what they don't want, no matter how much they might suspect that they need it. They vote with their feet. Many organisers, impatient of delay and anxious to get on with the job and give people something that is 'good for them', by-pass the slow and painstaking exercise of shared reflection, of teasing things out, of discovering priorities, of distinguishing the possible from the desirable.

One must not be blind to the fact, also, that the planning group may arrive at the wrong answer. They may be so impressed by the forthright opinions of some of their members that they eventually accept what is proposed, even though they do not wholeheartedly agree with it. For example, one member could insist that the introduction of prayer groups in the parish would meet all the needs. Because everyone is aware of the importance of prayer, and most realise they are not all that devoted to it, they feel less free in opposing the suggestion. For unexpressed reasons an incorrect decision may be taken. However, this is less likely to happen if care has been taken in the selection of members of the planning group.

Consult the people

It is possible to devise a number of ways in which the people could be directly consulted. A questionnaire distributed at Sunday Mass, which every parishioner is invited to complete, would give a parish planning group a fair indication of what would interest the parishioners. This procedure is, of course, open to the accusation that it is a manipulative technique; that the needs of the parishioners are being prescribed rather than elicited. The planners who drew up the questionnaire are in a way suggesting that it is in these particular areas, and not in others, that the interests of the parishioners lie. However, if in the opinion of the planners certain needs would be genuinely recognised, genuinely felt as needs, when brought to the awareness of the parishioners through the questionnaire, then the people have been consulted.

The disadvantage of the questionnaire method is, however, that although it can be said that the parishioners have been 'consulted', there is no genuine exchange of views between planners and parishioners. To achieve this is not an easy matter. A general invitation to the entire parish to meet to 'discuss' the matter could so easily result in the vociferous or the opinionated few dictating the conclusions arrived at. There are, however, ways of conducting an open meeting of parishioners that could minimise the obvious hazards, and secure that at least a general idea of what people wanted would emerge.

A particular questionnaire, let us say, would seem to indicate five definite topics of interest. Should the planning group settle for these and straight away invite five experts to speak on the topics in the parish hall? It is not as simple as that. Behind each of these five questions is a whole area of theological thinking stemming from scripture, developed through the Church's history, and with cultural overtones.

The planning group must know how to analyse the returns; how to discern what lies behind the particular topic, and why it has been selected. Suppose, for instance, one of the questions is 'What really happens at Baptism?' The interest in this question could be interpreted as a request for some instruction on the sacrament, or on the New Rite of Baptism. On the other hand, it may have arisen because the parish clergy have recently made some difficulty about baptising children whose parents are known to have ceased practising their religion, and this has given rise to a good deal of local anxiety. If this is so, then the reason behind the request, the 'need', is to allay their own anxiety. This could come through a better understanding of Original Sin, of grace and the sacrament — even of Church.

There is another method of discovering people's needs and wants which has more to recommend it. First of all, nine to twelve volunteers in the parish are recruited in response to a request from the pulpit. At a meeting they would be given the task simply of 'listening' to people — at bus stops, in supermarket queues, in pubs, wherever people meet each other. They would be asked to note the hopes and fears, the anxieties that they heard expressed,[1] and report these to the planning group. A list could then be drawn up and priorities would emerge. This method has the advantage over the others mentioned in that the context is the world of ordinary life, and the responses are not conditioned by the 'church' context.

Summary

1. The planning group should research the religious educational needs and wants of the local adult community.
2. It should not settle for quick answers or facile solutions.
3. It should evaluate the findings of its research into people's needs and wants to ensure real understanding of what is being asked.

Figure 2

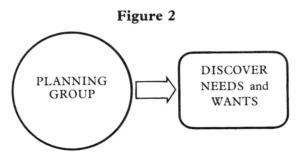

NOTES

1. This method was used with great success in the East London pastoral area of the Diocese of Westminster in 1979-80. Forty-two parishes co-operated in the project.

Translate into general aims

THE planning group have now by one means or another discovered the needs and wants. They have agreed on one of these as a priority. The next stage is for them to formulate in general terms what they intend to do in relation to the agreed priority, and why they are doing it.

In Egan/Cowan, this statement of general aims is described as a 'mission statement'. An expedition to climb Mount Everest or to reach the North Pole is described as a mission. Foreign ministers go on peace missions. We all understand the significance of the term. Mission implies more than just a statement of interest: it embodies the values, the philosophy, the reason why the operation is being undertaken.

Whether we use the term 'general aims' or 'mission statement', this is the point at which the planning group have to decide what they intend to offer as a service to the people they have consulted, and why. They must be honest enough to recognise that there could be a temptation to impose their own translation on the statement of needs and wants that has been made to them; to manipulate it in a particular direction just because this appeals to them personally. They must also avoid coming up with a mission statement that is so vague, theoretical and imprecise that almost any programme could come from it.

An example or two may serve to show the importance of getting this course of action right. Take St Mary's Parish. A planning group have honestly attempted to discover the felt needs and wants in their area, a down-town district with large numbers of unemployed, especially among the youth, and a fairly large black community. The statement of needs and wants has come up as: 1. Racialism: What can I do in my neighbourhood? 2. Youth unemployment: How can I help? 3. Attitudes to property: When is it stealing? When is it borrowing? After much discussion, the planning group agree to tackle the third of these. Parents, having been involved in the preparation of their children for the Sacrament of Reconciliation, begin to show real anxiety. A conflict surfaces between their parental role of bringing up their children to be honest and their own work practices in relation to 'borrowing', 'knocking off', 'stealing'. The mission statement first produced by the planning group is: 'To enable the parents to recognise the primacy of their moral judgement, to understand moral principles and to apply them in their own work situations'. Aha! you will be saying — as someone in the planning group is bound to point out — the influence of intellectuals is evident in the language of this statement. It needs to be restated in simpler terms. The corrected version comes out:

'To help parents in matters concerning themselves to answer the question "How do I know I'm right?"'

Of course this will benefit the children indirectly; although this is not part of the general aim.

Now take St Joseph's Parish. The liturgy planning group have met and concluded from a careful assessment of needs and wants in the parish that the priority would be a deeper understanding of the Scriptures as the Word of God speaking to the individual personally. Their general aim is stated, accordingly:

'To enable members of the parish to recognise and understand the Word of God speaking to them in their personal and social lives.'

It is important that such a statement of general aims be agreed and recorded in writing for the benefit, in the first instance, of the members of the planning group. It should also be passed on to all who later may come in, whether they come to help or to take part.

It may sound very simple; but in practice it is always tempting to by-pass this stage in the planning process. The result would then be a hit-and-miss approach, with neither planners nor participants being clear what they are about, even in general terms. This would weaken motivation and lead to frustration; while those keen enough to persevere would feel somehow that while the thing on offer in the parish isn't *really* what they want or need, maybe they'll go along with it just to keep Father happy.

Summary

The planning group should translate the needs and wants into a statement of general aims:

— what they intend to do; and
— why they are doing it.

Figure 3

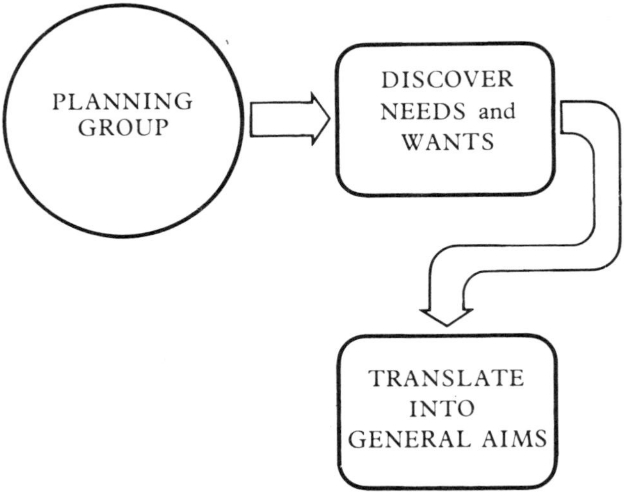

Develop into specific goals

OF ALL the stages in the planning process, the next is probably the most difficult but in the long term probably the most worthwhile.

The members of the planning group, having decided what are their general aims, must ask themselves the question: what do we hope to accomplish by the activity we are planning? In the light of these general aims what are our goals?

Passing an examination is a goal. So is learning to drive; giving up smoking; losing weight; going to the Holy Land. How we do these things is another matter, but it stands to reason that before we get involved in practical details we must be clear about what we hope to accomplish. Egan/Cowan[1] advise us that goals should be:

- *Behavioural,* clear, concrete, specific, operational;
- *Measurable,* or at least verifiable so that it is clear when they have been accomplished;
- *Realistic,* not set too high, capable of being accomplished with available resources;
- *Worthwhile,* not set too low, not petty or meaningless; and
- *Adequate,* i.e., goals that satisfy real needs and wants.

Let us suppose, for instance, that the diocese is deeply in debt, and that the finance committee have been instructed to devise some ways of raising money. A meeting of the committee is called. The members who attend have all given a good deal of thought to the problem, and several have come to the meeting prepared to offer suggestions on how the necessary money could be raised. To one it is a simple matter of increasing the diocesan levy on the parishes. Another is convinced that he can use his influence with the local radio station to have a broadcast appeal for contributions. A third has the bright idea of designing and marketing a diocesan T-shirt. The chairman, quite rightly, reminds the members that before any of these suggestions is considered, they should be clear on one particular matter: what is it that they hope to achieve by their fund-raising efforts? What is their goal? After a good deal of discussion they agree that they should aim at raising about £50,000 by some means or other, and that they should do this within the next twelve months. The 'goal' is then stated as:

'Within the next twelve months to raise the sum of £50,000 for the diocese'.

The goal, as stated, is:

— clear, concrete and specific;
— measurable;
— realistic, i.e., it is capable of being accomplished with the resources available;
— Adequate, i.e., it should contribute in some meaningful way to the reduction of the diocesan debt;
— worthwhile, i.e., it is within the espoused values of the diocese;
— and it can be attained within a reasonable time frame.

Only now do the Committee proceed to consider the various suggestions of the members on how the goal should be achieved.

Let us take another example. St Bernadette's Parish is in a pastoral area where there is a good ecumenical climate, thanks to the efforts of the bishop and the leaders of the other churches. In this parish many of the people have expressed the desire to be more actively involved, so that ecumenism becomes more than a mere reflection of the climate. The expressed *need and want* of the people could in this instance be said to be personal:

'What we want to do to further ecumenism';

and also apostolic:

'what we think needs to be done about church relations within and for the area'.

As a first step the parish has recently formed an ecumenical group of nine people with the *general aim* or mission statement:

'to foster inter-church relations within the area'.

All nine members are Catholic, though four of them have non-Catholic partners and one a non-Christian partner. After two exploratory meetings ranging over a whole host of possible plans and projects, all the members agree that first and foremost they need to have a clear and up to date understanding of salvation within the Catholic tradition. The group conclude that all the sympathy, openness, tolerance and appreciation in the world of other traditions would not be well grounded without a clear grasp of this. So the immediate need of the group is beginning to show itself. They have other needs, such as, for example, knowing the way the other Christian bodies understand salvation, Church, sacraments, etc. But the most urgent need is the one named above. In the minutes of the meeting the *major aim* reads as follows:

'As a group we intend as a first step in our ecumenical activity to gain a clear and deep knowledge of the Catholic Church's understanding of salvation'.

Before dispersing they agree to reflect on this aim and think about ways of making it more concrete. When the group reassemble it does not take long for ideas to surface. A clear point that emerges is that an understanding of salvation also has to include some examination of related topics such as grace, sin, baptism, Church. It takes some time and much effort to shape all these reflections into clear, concrete, specific goals. However, the group have enough sense to see that without this exercise their whole endeavour for ecumenism will be vague, woolly and ineffective, even sentimental. So the goal is now recorded in the minutes of the meeting:

'Catholic belief and teaching on salvation specifically in relation to grace, sin, baptism and Church to be explored and clearly understood within six months'.

This goal is *clear and specific*. 'Understanding achieved' is a specific accomplishment. The members of the group will know whether they have attained the knowledge or not, whether they are clear and feel they can handle it. The goal is *realistic* because it is within the capacity of the group. It is *adequate,* in that it satisfies the priority need felt and expressed by the group. It is also consonant with the values of the members and so could be said to be *worthwhile.* Finally the goal is set in a reasonable *time-frame* bearing in mind the task of the ecumenical group.

Summary

The planning group develop their aim(s) into goal(s) which should be clear, specific, concrete, measurable, realistic, worthwhile, adequate, within a time-frame.

Figure 4

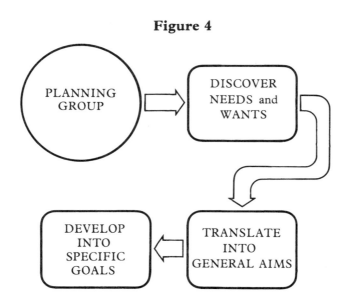

NOTES

1. Egan/Cowan, op cit p126.

Shaping the final project

WHEN goals have been clearly set, planning groups have to choose the right means to attain them. They have to decide the best course of action to follow. They have also to bear in mind that each stage of the action requires to be planned and shaped.

Let us return to the ecumenical planning group whom we left at the end of the last chapter at the point where they have agreed on their goal. Having clarified their goal, it becomes obvious to the group that

'theological help in some shape or form must be secured'.

This then becomes a *sub-goal* to be dealt with first. To discover what kind of theological help will serve them best, they decide to use the brainstorming technique. This method leaves the outcome wide open by accepting randomly all ideas put forward. The brainstorming, as expected, produces a wide range of suggestions, including several theologians, Fathers A, B and C, Sisters D and E, Mr F, Ms G, heads of RE from local schools, the parish priest, a theologian from the diocesan seminary, Vatican II Documents, UNI tapes, A New Catechism ...

The suggestions coming from the brainstorm are pruned along these lines. Which of them would not be practical? Of those left, which are unlikely to meet our needs? The few that remain all indicate a person. The discussion now centres on what sort of person they are looking for. A theologian? What does the term mean? Someone who teaches theology, or who writes on theological subjects? Must this person be a priest? Isn't it true that not just any theologian would do, but only someone who has made a special study or shown a special interest in this particular field? Is theological knowledge all they are looking for? Mustn't the person they select be able to relate easily to people, to discuss, not just to expound? Where are they likely to find their person? On the staff of the diocesan seminary? In a college of education? On a school staff? In the parish? Among the members of one of the local religious communities? Or...?

How do they go about finding this person? Here immediately is another *sub-goal*, the stages towards achieving which must now be named and shaped.

- *Name* as many persons as come to mind — laymen, laywomen, priests, sisters, brothers — who are competent theologically and can work well in and with a group.
- *Consider* these one by one. So-and-so is a brilliant speaker, television panel person; but is he the sort of person they can talk to? Would he listen? Another lives rather too far away; probably would not be able to attend their meetings at times suitable to them. A third is not a particularly exciting person, but she would appreciate the importance of what they are doing.
- *Select* three names in order of preference.
- *Describe the job:*
  - ☐ To work with the group, enabling them to achieve the goal of exploring and understanding Catholic belief and teaching on salvation, especially in relation to grace, sin, baptism and church, as a first step in their general aim of fostering ecumenical activity in the area.
  - ☐ To attend group meetings (not more than twelve, not fewer than ten), each approximately two hours, within a period of six months.
  - ☐ Remuneration to be in accordance with local education authority scale of professional fees.
- *Decide mode of approach:*
  - ☐ The chairperson to write to the theologian of first choice describing the major aim and goal of the ecumenical group, the approximate time commitments, i.e., length and number of meetings, and inviting him/her to consider putting his/her expertise at the service of the group; the chairperson should specify the remuneration agreed by the group. If he/she should decline, the chairperson to approach the second and third choice in the same way.
  - ☐ Having secured the theologian, the chairperson to invite him/her to the next meeting of the ecumenical group to work out in detail the content programme for the next six months.

This will include a breakdown and shaping of the content and agreement on the shape of the meetings.

The group, now including the theologian, are ready to consider the procedure for achieving the main goal; namely, that Catholic belief and teaching on salvation, specifically in relation to grace, sin, baptism and church, be explored and clearly understood within six months. They proceed as follows:

1. During the first meeting, at the suggestion of the theologian, they use the brainstorming technique on the key words in the goal: salvation, grace, sin, baptism, church. This enables the theologian to have some idea where they are, theologically. Brainstorming is used to keep the planning initiative for the content in the hands of the group.
Some of the things thrown in are:

— Salvation from what?
— 'Outside the Church no salvation'.
— 'Christ died for all'.
— How necessary is Baptism?
— 'Unless a man is born of water ...'
— Grace — what is it?
— No Baptism — no grace?
— What about Gandhi?
— Original Sin — my sin?
— Adam and Eve — what are we to believe?
— What's so special about being a Catholic?

2. The theologian, using his/her group skills and theology, helps them to analyse the results of the brainstorming and order the points into some kind of priority. In doing this they pay particular attention to ensuring that areas of difficulty on their side are matched with areas of doctrinal development coming from him/her. The result is ten clear topics.

Why so much time given to this? Why not let the theologian decide to make his/her own list of content for the meetings? Simply because theologising is reflecting on a way of life, and the very shaping of the contents with the help of the theologian is in itself 'doing theology'. This is a joint operation. The exercise is enriching for both the group and the theologian. What use is the science of theology if it becomes removed in content, style and language from those who live the

Christian life and wish to understand more fully the beliefs implicit in it.

3. The members of the group contract to meet eleven times at fortnightly intervals. They feel that at least two weeks should elapse between meetings. This is to allow sufficient time to do the reading, to reflect on and absorb the revised ideas which would challenge existing understanding and attitudes, giving rise to new questions from their own experience.

4. The theologian requires each member to agree to some prescribed reading. 'I can't work, unless you prepare.'

- Each member to have access to a Bible and copy of Documents of Vatican II.
- Each person contracts to read the prescribed passages in preparation for each meeting;
- to note down areas of difficulty;
- to note down at least one life experience called to mind by the reading.

5. The group now lay down their conditions for the procedure to be followed at each meeting. 'What kind of meeting do we want?' they ask. One which gives maximum opportunity for participation, because the goal of 'exploring' and 'better understanding' requires participation. Having clarified this, they agree a two hour time-frame and the following *shape* for each session:

- The theologian briefly to unfold the topic (20 mins).
- He/she to open the discussion and involve the group in exploring the topic (40 mins).
- Tea/coffee break (15 mins).
- Members encouraged to bring forward matters still requiring clarification, noted down in their preparatory reading and from reflection on life experience (30 mins).
- Preparation for next meeting (5 mins).
- Quick evaluation: How did the meeting go? (5 mins).
- Prayer (5 mins).

⋆　⋆　⋆

This chapter has dealt so far with the problem facing one particular group in shaping their project from general aims and goals. The size of the ecumenical group, nine persons in all, makes the setting-up of the project easier in this particular instance. But it could happen, and usually does, that a planning group are concerned to organise a project involving a much larger number of people — possibly even the entire adult population of a parish. In such a situation an added consideration would be the publicity necessary to bring the project to the attention of the larger numbers; and here publicity is of the essence. A strange characteristic of most Church and charitable organisations seems to be the somewhat naïve assumption — we are tempted to say presumption — that once something is planned people will come.

Figure 5

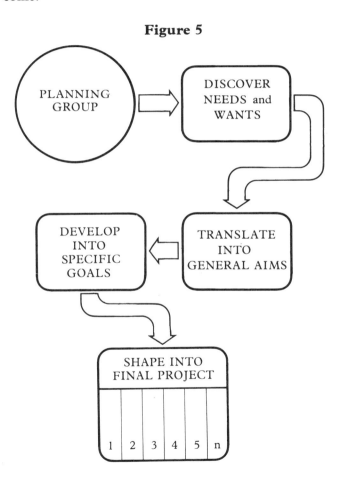

Working knowledge and skills

THE MOST valuable resource in any adult religious education project is people, both those who are involved in organisation and administration and those participating.

Participants apart, most parishes have far more qualified personnel with the necessary *working knowledge* than at first sight is apparent. An investigation of what is available invariably causes surprise. A parish priest or curate, preferably from another parish, might already be known to have an interest; might even be something of a specialist in a particular field of religious studies. He might equally be qualified as a lawyer, be a member of the diocesan justice and peace commission, or a speaker for CIIR or CND. Occasionally a priest is also a qualified social worker or counsellor.

A parish will often have some people with special qualifications of a different kind — journalists, for instance, or members of the local borough council; a local Member of Parliament, perhaps; a CMAC counsellor, a professional social worker, a shop steward, an industrial training officer, a communication skills training consultant: the list is endless. These people will not feel they are experts on adult religious education, but in their own particular field they are capable of making an outstanding contribution.

Communities of religious sisters or brothers in a parish or neighbourhood can also be counted on. Today it is quite common for religious men and women to have some special qualification in theology or pastoral studies in addition to a professional qualification as a teacher, nurse or social worker, with all the accompanying skills.

On the principle that people should not be asked to perform any task for which they have not the necessary working knowledge or *skills,* it is essential to check out among these knowledgeable people, which of them are good communicators. All the knowledge in the world is of little use in this context without good communication skills. What, in this context is a good communicator? Principally, a person who can share information rather than just impart it. To be able to do this effectively he/she must be skilled in the art of listening, whether on a one-to-one basis or in the group. Such a person 'hears' the fear, the conviction, the feeling, the uncertainty, the anger behind the words. Listening therefore includes empathy, an openness to the other, to what he/she is trying to communicate, either as a query or a response. However, offering support through good listening is not enough. Knowing how and where to challenge is also necessary to keep the group engaged on the task. Finally, the good communicator encourages feedback, creating a climate where the group are able to express negative criticism as well as positive appreciation.

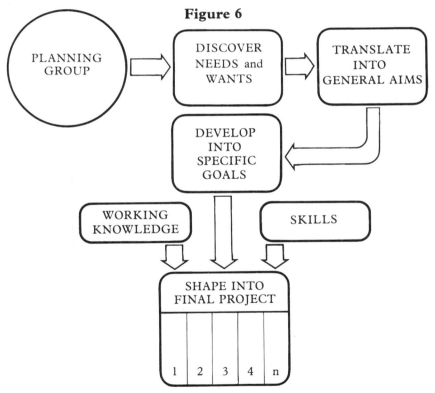

Figure 6

It is worthwhile adding that though communication skills are important, they are no substitute for the quality of the person using them. Adult religious education projects based largely on volunteers often collapse simply because in time the volunteers realise that they are inadequately equipped for the task — they lack the necessary knowledge or skills or both. No amount of generous commitment can compensate for these deficiencies.

Other resources

IT IS ALSO necessary to take stock of the other resources that are needed and make sure they will be available at the times when they are wanted. Is there a parish hall or social centre which can be used for group meetings? Is there a Church of England or Free Church hall or social centre in the area where rooms could be hired? Is there a local authority adult education centre or evening institute, institute of further education, college of education or university extra-mural study centre in the parish or in the area? Is there a primary or secondary school within the neighbourhood; and has the school shown any interest in community education?

In deciding to use any of these places, preference should be given — other things being equal — to those which provide access for the disabled. If any of these is willing to allow one of its spaces to be hired for an adult religious education session, would it also allow some of its equipment to be made available, e.g., blackboard (including chalk and duster), flip chart, film strip, film projector (with lamps in working order!), tape recorder, TV for video, overhead projector? (Even so, you would be advised to bring with you an extension lead and a plug adaptor.)

Socialising at refreshment time can be an integral part of the programme (but only, alas, if the necessary equipment is available and in working order. Assurance is not enough — always check!).

Finally, a 'transport co-operative', a parish minibus or car-sharing, though important resources in themselves, are in fact much more. They can foster community, sharing, neighbourliness. They often bring to the sessions those who otherwise would not venture to come — the disabled, and those afraid of mugging.

Summary

- The planning group will shape the agreed goals into a final project.
- They will define clearly and shape the steps or stages by which each goal will be achieved.
- They will carefully select knowledgeable and skilled people to be responsible for the conduct of any part of the adult religious education project.
- They will take stock of the other resources available, and will agree on which of these are to be used, and how.

'People working together on a project have to decide who does what and how.'

The planning group: further implications

IT IS OBVIOUS that people working together on a project have at some stage to decide who does what and how. In other words, a structure is necessary and roles and tasks must be clear. Let us see what this would mean in practice.

Someone must undertake to see that the hall, or the place for the meeting, is open in good time, and that the seating is suitably arranged. This may involve contacting a caretaker and making sure that he/she has not forgotten the fixture; and, if it is winter, that the heating is turned on and that the lavatories are opened and indicated. If refreshments are being offered, this also must be prearranged, checking that there is a kettle or urn in working condition. All this may seem very trivial and something that could be taken for granted; but any infant teacher would tell you that a good lesson is often spoiled by such a simple matter as a lack of sharpened pencils.

Hospitality is a special role and cannot be left to chance. It is important that the shy, the diffident, the newcomers are made to feel at home. If there is registration, someone must be detailed to enrol the applicants. If there is a course fee (and experience leads us to recommend that there should be), it is someone's role to receive and 'bank' the money. If books are on offer, sale return or borrow, again it has to be someone's special responsibility; preferably someone interested in books and who has some measure of business acumen.

If the programme requires the use of any equipment, then immediately a series of roles is involved: who provides, collects, operates, checks and returns it.

Finally there is the role of the chairperson. Success in any meeting depends a lot on the chairperson. It is not an easy thing to be in charge of a meeting without seeming to be, to conduct the discussion in such a manner that no one feels there is such a thing as a foolish question, to sum up in such a way that the central message of the speaker is clarified and underlined.

Relationships must be clear

The distribution of roles within a structure implies and causes relationships. However, these relationships are primarily with a view to the efficient and effective carrying out of the work. All members of the planning group, who may be good friends, should be clear in their own minds about this. An example may help. Someone whose role is publicity has been detailed to write an article for inclusion in the local press. He should feel entitled to do just this. He should not therefore feel it necessary to submit the article for approval to anyone before publication; not even to the chairperson of the planning group. To do so would be to abdicate the power that comes to him/her with the brief of being responsible for publicity. It would queer the role of chairperson, forcing him/her to assume the role of supervisor, with all the relational complications that would arise.

Communication must be encouraged

Apart from the building of community, which the Church is all about, communication is concerned, also, as with any system, with getting a job done well. So the sharing of information, of ideas, of apprehensions and misgivings, of criticism, should be positively encouraged among all members, whether planners, organisers or participants, in any adult religious education venture. Withholding of opinions and ideas in the context of adult religious education is usually due more to shyness, fear of authority figures and lack of experience, than to motives of power, prestige or competitiveness.

Equally important is information in the shape of feedback, or 'ongoing evaluation', to use the current technical term. This simply means, as the term implies, that all concerned, whether as planners or participants, have a clear idea of what they are about, and are positively encouraged to take a critical look at every stage of the action and at themselves as they go through it, and to be willing to share their observations, feelings and criticisms. Instead of waiting till the end to ask what went wrong, or why it succeeded, all should be encouraged to remodel, adjust, prune, even change their own contribution and the project itself.

A good atmosphere is important

Organisations, like families, differ enormously, particularly in the quality of their shared life. When you are with them, even for a short time, you become conscious of a climate, an atmosphere. It is something you feel rather than know how to define. The same could be said of a school, an office, a factory, a parish, and equally a planning group.

It is a good thing to be aware of the factors that go to make a bad or good climate; bad or good in so far as it helps an organisation to achieve its purpose or hinders it. When there is a poor climate one finds distrust, suspicion and competitiveness between members, instead of trust and collaboration; each one pursuing selfish interest rather than working for the common good; each one shrinking into a protective shell rather than risk the hazards of open disagreements; lifeless and dispirited responses to an impersonal authority rather than a feeling that opinions are welcomed and that honest, friendly argument precedes the making of decisions.

Don't forget the environment

Organisations do not work in isolation. They are always in a particular place and cultural context, where all sorts of other organisations are at work. All planners and participants are influenced by, and can influence, these in their turn. Look, for instance, at the church environment, the local parish. Here the planning group would need to be aware of the parish clergy, the parish council, the schools, racial mix, the other Christian and non-Christian bodies. Aware also of the employment pattern, with part-time and shift systems, the social class pattern in the area, the political flavour, the subcultures, even the geography and the eating habits, the transport system and, over all, the mass media and its impact. All these must be considered. They can be a help or a hindrance. What is important is that the planning group are aware and take their influence into account. To fail to do so would be to risk a build-up of all sorts of environmental stress in the form of opposition, apathy or indifference.

Here, finally, is a model for the adult religious education planning process.

Figure 7

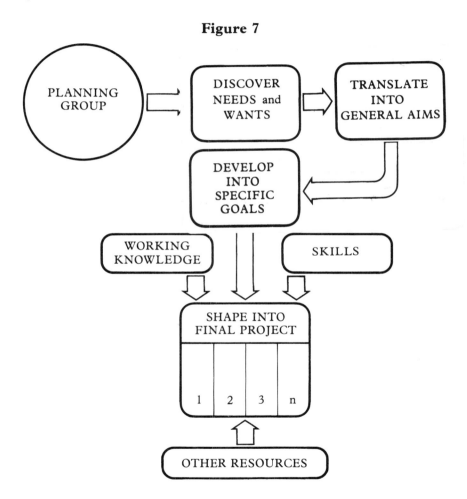

PART THREE

Twenty ways of doing it

IF ADULT religious education is considered to be so important, so necessary in the modern Church, what is being done to provide it? The answer is: if one looks for diocesan or regional planning, then not a great deal is happening; although it should immediately be added that what is actually being done seems to have an enormous significance for the future. However, planning or organising apart, when one looks around to see what initiatives are appearing, one is struck by their multiplicity, richness and variety. These very initiatives are the most startling and encouraging tribute to the need that is felt for this particular service.

If we enquire what is happening in other countries, we find that the variety of experiment is incredible. In the English-speaking countries alone — in the United States, Ireland, Canada, Australia and New Zealand — local circumstances have dictated such a difference of approach that it would be difficult to give a coherent account of it, and it would not be easy to adapt their different programmes for use elsewhere. In the Catholic communities of Europe the variety is even more pronounced. In the Rhineland and Austria the Catholic authorities have made extensive and imaginative use of the state television service to bring their adult religious education programmes to the people — something that would hardly be possible in Britain at present.

The purpose of Part Three of this book is to present the programme of one English diocese, Westminster. Westminster is unique in English dioceses in that it has had since 1975 a diocesan committee for adult education, and an adult education centre as the executive arm of the committee. In 1980 the committee discussed and approved a programme of adult religious education to be implemented in the course of the next few years. This programme listed twenty 'ways in which adults learn', some of which had been researched and proved successful, others being included as possible future experiments. The adult education committee instructed the officers of the diocesan centre to use all twenty. It is interesting as a blue-print of what one English diocese decided to do in the area of adult religious education. Here are the twenty:

1: Groups

Home-based groups

THESE are groups of around eight to twelve adults, meeting regularly by arrangement in one another's homes, in a parish centre, in a school, or a public house. Every group should have a trained person, a catechist of sorts, as a regular member. He or she can be a teacher, a priest or religious; a person who has in some way acquired training or qualification in religious studies. The presence of such a person in the group is an assurance to the members that they are dealing with the teaching of the Church at some depth. Nothing will be more likely to dishearten the group than the feeling that their discussions are little better than a pooling of common ignorance.

It is difficult to get the proper label which best describes the role of the trained person. 'Leader' has an overtone of superiority, of dominance, which is unacceptable here. 'Tutor' is somewhat better: if the group is a sort of seminar, and as a seminar is unthinkable without a tutor, then the trained person is the nearest thing to a tutor. But again there are academic overtones in these terms which would render them not quite suitable. 'Facilitator' is about the best description, implying a type of leadership that might be described as 'leadership from behind', a tutorship if you wish, but without suggesting any teacher-pupil attitude; someone whose function it is to feed in ideas, to stimulate but not direct the thinking, and in the process also to learn.

The topics for discussion could be agreed from one meeting to another. Alternatively, they could stem from an occasional talk given by a visiting speaker to members of all the groups together in a parish or church hall.

The small group when properly constituted is an ideal setting for a great deal of what is covered by the term 'adult education', and this is no less true when the subject is Christianity than when a non-religious subject is being studied. In a group discussion, individuals can be led to examine, discuss, reflect on and articulate, and finally recognise and begin to evaluate, their religious attitudes and assumptions. Growth in faith, transformation of the person — 'let this mind be in you, which was also in Christ Jesus' — is what is hoped for.

A group meeting lasts for approximately an hour and a half. Hospitality provided by the hostess is limited strictly to tea and biscuits. All sorts of complications arise from failure to keep to this simple rule. People silently, and for no apparent reason, drift away. The meetings take place about once a month, or once every three weeks, or as the group decide. When the group meet, to discuss, to share ideas, to learn together, the pay-off for the individual member is not just that he/she knows more about the subject, but that faith is deepened through this exchange, this sharing.

Groups when constituted should not go on and on indefinitely. As a rule group members are pleased rather than otherwise if at the beginning it is made clear that they commit themselves for a fixed period of time, maybe a year, at the conclusion of which the group is disbanded.

One reason why the group should not exceed twelve people is that with a greater number it is next to impossible to maintain one single open discussion for an hour and a half. The whole purpose of the meeting will be vitiated if everyone is not involved, or if the discussion is fragmented, or if two or three of the members take over and debate with each other while the rest listen. Members should feel able to speak their minds freely and without waiting to be called on to do so. They should also listen carefully to others, let them speak, too; and they should try to make the discussion pleasant for all. At no time during the discussion should there be any private conversation between members. No one person should be allowed to dominate the discussion. If this should begin to happen there are two good ways, among others, of dealing with the situation. One is to ensure that the person concerned sits next to the facilitator — leader. This invariably has the effect of stemming the flow. Another good method is to give him/her a task to perform, for example to write a note of the points raised as the discussion unfolds.

At some time during the meeting there should be prayer. This prayer may arise, for example, from reflection on an incident in the life of Our Lord, or following the discussion of something of special significance in the lives of the members. The prayer could be led by any one of the group members or by the facilitator. Towards the end of the meeting some attempt should be made to summarise the thinking of the group.

The meeting should end on time. There is a lot to be gained and seldom anything lost by a rigid adherence to the hour-and-a-half rule. Before they separate, the members should know the topic for discussion at the next meeting, and they should fix the date, time and place.

It should be clear by now that the family has a good deal to recommend it as the venue for these group meetings. People do not immediately feel at home in a room in a presbytery or in the parish centre, or in some other neutral setting, even in a convent. There are of course exceptional cases. On the other hand there are some disadvantages when meetings are held in what Vatican II calls 'the domestic church'. Frequent interruptions can come from the telephone; the doorbell; little children wanting drinks, the loo, a cuddle. Tensions can arise between the roles of hostess and leader: it is never easy to keep order in someone else's home. Even when the meeting closes, people tend to stay around. And there are some districts where people are understandably fearful of leaving their homes to go any distance on dark evenings for fear of mugging. This is where the individual group members must themselves decide what is best for most people.

Scripture study group

This is a special type of group. Members need not necessarily meet in someone's home, but all the evidence suggests that it is better if they do. In this group it is important that the facilitator should make a special study of the scriptural passages that are being examined. He/she might even, if the other members of the group are willing, assume the role of tutor.

Neighbourhood Mass

This has many of the characteristics of the home-based group. The Mass is held as a rule on a weekday evening in someone's home. There is an open invitation to attend, usually conveyed through the parish clergy or parish council, to all and every one of the residents in a particular street or streets. The neighbourhood Mass differs from the ordinary weekday evening Mass in the parish church in its atmosphere of friendly informality, and in its involvement of all who are present in the liturgy. Occasionally there is discussion in addition to the homily, and often these two are mingled.

Family and social action[1]

This national organisation works through family groups, neighbourhood groups (common interest groups; action-in-work groups), of those interested in enabling the family to impart a Christian influence on its environment. Discussion at these group meetings is conducted on the see-judge-act procedure. The family and social action groups help to build community in the parish and neighbourhood, and give a positive support to the family so that it can fulfil its missionary vocation.

Prayer group

This group's function, as the title implies, is to promote prayer, not religious education. There is, however, in all prayer a 'content' element; there is 'mind' as well as 'heart'. Those who join prayer groups should have opportunities for growing in knowledge of their faith in addition to expressing that faith in prayer. The words of Pope John Paul sound a note of caution here: 'Do not allow these groups,' he wrote,[2] 'which are exceptional occasions for meeting others, and which are blessed with such riches of friendship and solidarity among the young, of joy and enthusiasm of reflection on events and facts — do not allow them to lack serious study of Christian doctrine. If they do, they will be in danger — a danger that has unfortunately proved only too real — of disappointing their members and also the church'.

NOTES

1. The Westminster FSA officer is at 23 Kensington Square, London, W8.
2. *Catechesi Tradendae,* par 47.

2: Courses

THE COURSE is, as the name implies, a series of talks/discussions on a topic or series of topics in a learning situation. In this context it is a programme of religious education drawn up with the aim of attracting adults who want to know more about their faith. The organisers should keep in mind that the courses have as their objective not just better informed Christians but mutual growth in faith of both organisers and participants.

In general there are two types of course:

The parish programme

The entire religious education of adults could, of course, be organised and provided on a parish basis; that is to say, by the parish clergy working with and through a parish council. For the Catholic the parish is the spiritual community into which he was baptised and through which he receives many of the graces that enable him to develop into a mature Christian. Most Catholics have a sense of commitment to their parish, of involvement in its activities and celebrations, and many have a deep loyalty to it.

Most lay organisations in England and Wales — there are more than a hundred — are generally parish-based. The St Vincent de Paul Society, Legion of Mary, Catholic Women's League, Union of Catholic Mothers, all operate as a rule through the parish structure. Wherever there is some new development, such as the New Catechumenate, or Family Faith, or Sharing the Faith groups, it generally takes place in a parish setting. What more natural, therefore, than that adult religious education in its entirety should also be located here?

Many parishes are already doing a great deal in this particular field. The usual pattern is that speakers are invited to give talks in the parish hall or parish school hall on topics of interest to the parishioners. The speakers for these programmes, whether lay, religious, or members of the clergy, could either be from the parish or from a neighbouring parish. In addition to the advertised talk by the speaker, there is usually a question period at the end, an 'open forum' during which discussion can take place. Such a parish service of religious education for its members can be drawn up on an annual basis, and become a regular feature of parish life: it could provide the 'content' element for parish-based small group discussions.

The 'evening class'

The religious education programme could also be organised and conducted on the model of a local authority adult education course in an evening institute or adult education centre. It could also with much profit to the organisers be located in such a local authority adult institute or centre. In this case the added advantage is the ecumenical dimension. Alternatively, it could be based in a Catholic comprehensive school serving the parishes of a deanery from which children attend the school. There are two types of course of this nature. The first is the 'evening class' proper. This consists of some ten or twelve meetings on consecutive week-day evenings, running as

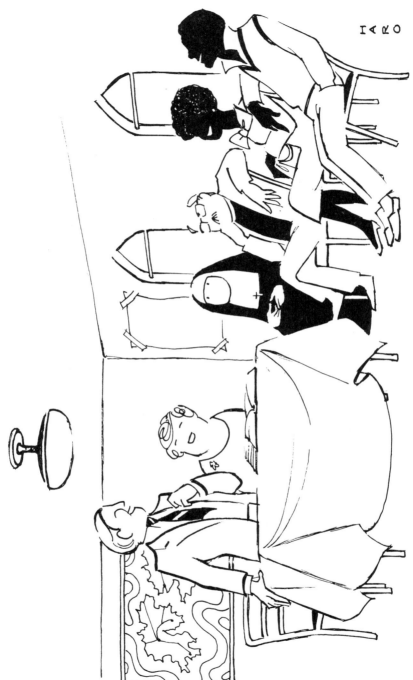

'Speakers are invited to give talks in the parish hall on topics of interest to the parishioners.'

a rule either from September to December or from January to March. Each meeting would last for approximately two hours. The ten or twelve topics on the course might each be dealt with by a different speaker, or there could be fewer speakers, or just one.

The procedure is usually something like this. The speaker is introduced, or introduces himself, and he or she then speaks on the topic for about thirty minutes. If there is to be a tea break, and it is strongly recommended that there should be, it could occur at this point, after which the audience breaks up into groups of eight, ten or twelve, each with a 'leader', to discuss the topic as presented by the speaker. Back then to the speaker for a plenary session lasting for about half an hour, where people put questions directly or ask for further explanation of some point. To be avoided at all costs in this final session is the formal 'reporting back' by the group leaders. Not only does this inhibit the development of any spontaneous open discussion of issues that have surfaced in the groups, but it risks the distortion even of what was discussed in the groups.

Ideally a library should be provided to accompany the course. The library should include books recommended by the speakers, in sufficient quantity to enable them to be borrowed by those taking the course. If this should prove impossible, a brief reading list might be compiled to accompany each of the talks, and the people on the course be encouraged to ask their local library to acquire these titles.

The 'seminar course'

There is a second type of course favoured by the LEAs which could be described as the 'seminar' type. It normally runs to ten or twelve evening meetings, but on occasion might even be fewer, consisting perhaps of no more than six. The difference is that here there is only one single tutor, and the enrolment is restricted to a small group of not more than fifteen to eighteen people. The group proceeds from a short introductory talk at each meeting to an examination of the subject. The course can be based on a particular text book, or a number of related topics from a particular book, the aim being to involve members in reading, preparing and eventually even introducing the subject for discussion. This type of course is probably best as a 'follow-on' to the previous one. As the 'evening class' type of course would probably draw on some five or six parishes for its membership, one could envisage a 'seminar' course being set up immediately in one or more of those parishes, at which a smaller number of people would study in some depth one or more topics from the programme of the course that had been concluded. There is no reason why this course should not lead to an O or A level qualification.

If a central theme is desirable, the subject matter of the programme, the content, will in a general way be contained in one or other of these five areas of the Church's belief and practice — scripture, morals, Church history, doctrine, liturgy and spirituality.

University extra-mural religious study courses

Courses

These courses normally operate in four different ways:

(i)   *The diploma or certificate course,* extending over four or three years respectively. Each year's course of twenty-four two-hour meetings is for students intending to pursue a preplanned course of religious studies, leading to the award of a diploma or a certificate by examination. Students are required to submit twelve units of individual work each year.

(ii) *The sessional course.* This comprises twenty-four two-hour meetings extending over the autumn and spring terms.

(iii) *The terminal course.* This normally extends over one term, with not more than twelve meetings, often on a specialist topic.

(iv) *The tutorial course* is a course of continuous study with the same tutor, normally of twenty-four two-hour meetings for three years.

In all these instances the speakers or tutors must be approved by the university.

The structured talk/discussion

This is simply the once-only 'special lecture' for a special occasion. The occasion could be the jubilee or patronal feast of the parish; a notable centenary celebration; the special interest of a Year of the Disabled or Year of the Elderly; the introduction of liturgical changes or new ministries (Eucharist) to the parish; a new sex education curriculum in the primary school, and so on. The procedure to be followed could be that recommended in the case of evening classes mentioned earlier in this chapter. Those attending the talk should be given an opportunity to discuss among themselves what the speaker has said and to raise questions for discussion.

3: Visual language: the use of film, film strip, video cassette

RELIGIOUS educational films and film strips have been on the market for many years now, and are widely used in schools. The video cassette is a relative newcomer in the field, but its educational potential, if properly exploited, is very great. More often than not these visual and audio-visual aids are used merely as adjuncts to a spoken lesson or lecture. The speaker uses them simply to contribute a visual dimension to his/her talk. Hence the word 'aid'. However, there is such a thing as visual language. In fact it is said that its increasing use will be as significant as was the printing press for the development of literacy. Visual language does not shore up the spoken or printed work; it has its own profound impact and has great potential for adult education whether overtly religious or not. As yet it has not been sufficiently researched to warrant other than recognition here.[1]

If a film or video cassette recording is to be used to present a religious topic to a group of adults it is recommended that:

☐ Its message should never be given in advance. To decide for an adult in advance what a particular image, or film or film strip, means, is to impose an interpretation as if it were the only acceptable one, and to imply that anything

☐ It should be shown first, without comment.

☐ The audience should then be divided into small groups, and each group asked to talk to one or two prepared questions designed to enable them to probe the inner meaning of what they have seen.

☐ The film could then be seen again.

☐ The viewers could be invited to share their insights with the entire group.

In the case of a *film strip*, with an accompanying text, the procedure is different. Here it is important to present the sequence of strips either in stages, or in their entirety, with their accompanying comments. At the end there should be open discussion.

NOTES

1. ACNAV — Association Catechetique Nationale pour l'Audio-Visuel, 6 Avenue Vavin, 75006 Paris.

4: Parish renewal

THE TERM 'parish renewal' was first used, it would appear, as the title of a scheme which originated in the United States in the early 1970s, and which has since been widely adopted in parishes in Ireland as well as in the United States. In spite of its title, the scheme did not attempt to involve the entire parish in a renewal exercise. It began with the assumption that the layman or laywoman in the pew could no longer be asked to attend the parish church morning and evening for a week or weeks on end, but that particular individuals would still be prepared to sacrifice an entire weekend on a one-off basis if there were a sufficiently good reason. On successive weekends, therefore, Friday evening to Sunday evening inclusive, groups of parishioners, twenty to fifty strong, are invited to attend a renewal programme and are taken through it by a priest assisted by two or three lay persons. The procedure has a lot in common with Marriage Encounter.

It is still possible, however, to involve the entire Mass-going parish in a renewal exercise, and there are three quite different ways in which this can be done.

Parish Renewal: Central London model[1]

The aim of the Central London project is to encourage growth in

Christian faith and living through prayer, teaching and reflection in faith, and practical action. The initial plan is to arrange a three-year programme of two six-week sessions a year. During this time the whole life of the parish becomes concentrated on certain aspects of Christian life and teaching through celebrating the liturgy, prayer, small group meetings and other events. The two six-week sessions take into account the fact that people are prepared to make some extra effort during the season of Lent. Again in the autumn most people, it is felt, would be prepared to commit themselves to this extra effort for a relatively brief period of time, when they know that the beginning and the end are well defined.

The programme is based on the Sunday Gospel readings. The three-year cycle of the Lectionary allows the key concepts presented in the Synoptic Gospels in the autumn session — the person of Christ (Mark), Christian living (Luke), the Church (Matthew) — to be used as special themes; and each of these can be developed in the following session in the Lenten readings.

In the course of each week of the two six-week Renewal periods, a number of activities are organised in the parish in which everyone is invited to take part. These could take the form of adult discussion groups, prayer groups, home-based liturgies, and so on. Those who take part in them are led to reflect again on the particular theme of the previous Sunday liturgy, to discuss, to pray, to share their insights, to consider how they should act on the Word they have received. If there should be a special 'area event' of any significance in the course of the week, such as a feast day, an exhibition or a religious assembly, these would also be used to celebrate the theme with the members of the local church involved. At the end of the sixth week of the session, which could be made to coincide with the Feast of Christ the King or with the Easter Vigil, there is a final liturgy in which the participants are led to make a personal renewal of commitment to the service of the Word.

There are a number of advantages in this Renewal procedure. Firstly, as the entire parish, indeed the whole area, is involved, this should help to build a sense of community within the area. The setting up of small group meetings should enable individual and local needs to become apparent; and this should result, further, in the discovery and use of individual gifts and, in the long term, the development of parish councils. Such a programme, if properly organised and presented, involves a good deal of initial planning. Fortunately the Bishop had the foresight to appoint full-time workers from the beginning to co-ordinate and promote the work. The co-operation and involvement of quite a number of parishioners in the exercise itself could provide a training experience and support for lay leadership.

Parish mission: new style

Another way to effect parish renewal is by means of a parish mission, but a parish mission with a difference. Every Roman Catholic adult knows what a parish mission is. It is an exercise undertaken by a parish on average every five to ten years, lasting on each occasion for from one to three weeks. Two or three priests from a religious order or missionary society visit the parish and, in the period of time at their disposal, conduct an intensive series of spiritual exercises, at the same time contacting every parish institution or society, visiting every home, and calling all to repentance and Christian renewal.

In our day, for a variety of reasons, the parish mission old style is being remodelled. However, the principle it embodied, the regular call to conversion and renewal, is still relevant. The special character of the parish mission, new style, is that the parish can operate it from start to finish without any assistance from outside sources. It can be a do-it-yourself exercise. The first step is to set up a parish planning group, ten or twelve people representative of every age range and every facet of parish life, under the chairmanship of the parish priest or a member of the parish clergy responsible to him.

The mission should not be of too long duration: a full week, Sunday to the following Sunday inclusive, would be sufficient. On each day one particular aspect of parish life would receive special consideration, so that the week-long programme might, among other possible alternatives, be something like this:

Opening Sunday: Parish Renewal Week launched. Special liturgies for principal morning and evening Masses highlighting the call to conversion inherent in the readings, supported by appropriate penitential rite, bidding prayers, hymns and music.

Family Day: Evening service devoted to families, married couples. Seder Meal. Ceremonial renewal of marriage vows.

Parish Life: Everyone involved. Film show: 'What is a Parish?' Discussion.

Reconciliation: Everyone involved. Special Rite. Confessions. Absolution.

The Eucharist in the life of the parish: Evening Mass. Special transport for parish elderly and handicapped.

Children's Day: Dramatic production by school children on Renewal theme, in the parish church or school hall.

Parish Life: Display of material showing history of parish, charts illustrating parishioners' occupations, impact of parish on its environment. Evening vigil, with parish societies attending for one hour in turn. Midnight Mass.

Closing Sunday: Again special liturgies. If possible, Baptism during Mass, adult or infant; reception of converts. In the evening, parish social. Everyone invited.

The Mission Team

Another way in which a Renewal programme could be conducted is through a mission team. The team in question is a group of priests, religious, laywomen and laymen who come together to plan and conduct a mission of renewal and offer it to a parish, a school, or to special groups, e.g. naval cadets, army barracks, nurses' training units, sixth-form colleges. Here is development of ministry, the visiting and all that goes with that experience — acceptance, rejection, indifference. The aim is not overtly to get people back to religious observance so much as to bring them the Good News, to incarnate to them the caring church, concerned to re-enkindle in them the flame of faith, to counter their feeling of irrelevance to life, of sheer drift.

The witness of the laity in the renewal and the growth of faith has often a powerful effect on those one-time believers who have now lapsed. A visit from a sister or lay person is often less threatening to some who have for too long thought of a priest as someone who 'wants me back' in church.

The 'mission' which the team conducts should also be completed within a limited time sequence — a fortnight at the longest. Each week there could be two special weekday evening meetings in a parish church or chapel, one concerned with Reconciliation, the other centred on the Eucharist.

NOTES

1. The Central London Area has adopted this programme based on a three-year cycle beginning September 1982.

'Some churches have commuter congregations at their weekday services.'

5: The mini-mission

SOME churches, for instance those in inner-city areas, have commuter congregations at their weekday services. Office workers, often in surprisingly large numbers, devote twenty-five minutes of a lunchtime one-hour break to attend Mass and receive Holy Communion. Here a new type of mission is indicated.[1]

The key to the successful planning of the mini-mission is the ability to add a five-minute mission homily to the weekday Mass without adding to the twenty-five minutes it takes to celebrate. If this condition is genuinely accepted and rigidly adhered to, then the mission programme could be:

☐ The parish clergy advertise the mission well in advance, and assist with Communion.

☐ Five special liturgies are composed for five successive Monday-to-Friday midweek or evening Masses, on the five themes of Christian Renewal — conversion of heart, reconciliation, prayer, Eucharist, mission.

☐ A special preacher for the homily at the five Masses.

☐ Confessions available after Mass.

☐ A leaflet summarising in an interesting way the main message of the homily, together with prayers and additional reflections, to be given to each person as he/she leaves church.

☐ Coffee and snacks in parish hall after the Friday Mass for those who wish.

☐ Finally, evaluation by priests and planners after the mission in preparation for successive ventures.

NOTES

1. Such a mini-mission was tried at three London inner-city parish churches in 1980 — St Patrick's, Soho, Holy Rosary, Marylebone, St Anselm's and St Cecilia's, Kingsway.

6: Catechesis based on liturgical seasons

WHILE it is encouraging that the number of people interested in adult religious education in recent years has increased and is increasing, it must be admitted that the number of those involved is still a minority of the community of believers. 'We have witnessed many excellent initiatives in the field of renewal; for example prayer groups, Bible study groups, the Charismatic movement, the growth of many new caring ministries, the lay missionary endeavour. But much of this activity is still the preserve of the minority. For the most part, such activities leave the man or woman in the pew unmoved. The level of involvement of many Catholics remains the fulfilment of the Sunday Mass obligation'.[1]

Then why not begin where people are, the congregation attending Mass in their parish church on Sunday morning? Accepting the fact that the function of liturgy is not primarily education but celebration, it should still be possible to avail of the educational and catechetical opportunities it offers, and in so doing integrate the other initiatives mentioned into the mainstream of parish life.

● To begin with, we have the three readings. These are usually from the Old Testament, the New Testament letters and the Gospel. Take a particular liturgical season, such as Advent, Lent or Pentecost. Discern the overall theme linking the successive Sunday

Readings, e.g. hope (Advent), reconciliation (Lent). The celebrant will make this theme the 'message' of his homily, illustrated and elaborated not only from the readings but also from the Psalms, the prayers, the final blessing of the Mass. The theme will also be echoed in the music, the hymns sung by choir and congregation, the bidding prayers.

● The celebrant could not, in the limited time available to him for his homily, attempt to fill in the historical context of the diverse writings or deal with the exegetical textual problems they present. Indeed, it would not be advisable for him to attempt to do so. There is no reason, however, why an opportunity to study such things could not be provided for those parishioners who would be interested, outside of Mass. A scripture study session could be held in the week before the appropriate Sunday to which everyone is invited. There, under the guidance of a scripture teacher, the readings could be examined and commented on.

● The special theme suggested by the readings could also be adopted for prayer group meditation. Prayer groups are nowadays a familiar feature of parish life. A ten-minute recorded meditation on the theme could be sent to prayer groups in the parish, to the liturgy team, to religious communities, to all those participating in the scheme.[2]

● The theme of the liturgical season and its elaboration in the homily of the previous Sunday Mass could also be taken as the subject to be used in the weekly parish catechism class.

● It might seem to ask a lot to suggest that the celebrant's homily delivered during the Sunday Mass might be planned in conjunction with the parishioners, but there are in fact some parishes[3] where this does take place. All that is required is an open invitation from the parish clergy to the parishioners to a meeting held regularly in the church or parish hall on a specific weekday evening to discuss the form and content of the following Sunday's homily. The laity who attend these meetings are quite able to spell out, for the benefit of the clergy, the special relevance of the readings to the parish community. During the class banners could be made by the children based on the liturgical theme. These would be blessed by the parish priest, hung in the parish church, and commented on during the following Sunday's liturgical celebrations.

An organised parish programme such as we have described would have the effect of linking the parish liturgy, study group, prayer groups, and children's catechism class in celebrating the liturgical season. Religious activities in the parish, hitherto isolated and fragmented, would in this way be truly integrated.

NOTES

1. *To Know the Mystery of Salvation,* by George Stack, *Liturgy* Vol 4 No 3. In his article Fr Stack describes in detail a catechetical project based on the Sunday liturgies of Advent which he planned and operated in conjunction with WAREC in the diocese of Westminster in 1979.
2. A series of such meditations was composed and tape recorded by Fr Alan Fudge to accompany Fr George Stack's 1979 Advent series.
3. e.g. St Anselm's, Southall, Middlesex.

7: Liturgy workshop

IN SIMPLE terms the workshop is a group of people which has been formed for the express purpose of giving expression through the creative arts — music, drama, movement, the visual arts — to a religious truth or truths presented for a particular liturgical occasion. The workshop is always an *ad hoc* creation. Some planning body has constituted it and given it a specific objective, a task to achieve. The planning body could be the parish liturgy committee, or a school staff, or the parish council itself. The workshop as constituted would normally include at least one person who had special qualifications or experience in music, drama, movement, or whatever is the art form which the project requires.

The type of project the liturgy workshop might be commissioned to produce could include:

— a choral speaking accompaniment to a Service of Reconciliation in the parish church;
— a mime illustrating a Gospel incident or an episode in the life of a Saint to introduce or accompany the liturgy of a Sunday Mass or patronal feast in the parish church;
— the offertory procession at a school Mass;
— the dramatisation by schoolchildren of a seasonal theme, such as sin and reconciliation in Lent; and
— the choral and orchestral accompaniment to a solemn confirmation in the parish church.

In both the planning and the execution of such projects there would necessarily be a great deal of religious and theological discussion which could be a powerful formation of attitudes for those participating. Those who take part in such activities could not fail to interiorise the attitudes suggested by the activity.

8: Away-day

AS THE TITLE indicates, this is an organised outing of a group of people, taking them away from their home environment for a period lasting some time between mid-morning and late evening. In its simplest form this could be a 'parish outing'; but there are many possible variations.

To avoid confusion, let us take two particular instances: that of a parish society such as the UCM or CWL arranging an annual away-day for its members, and a family away-day where parent and children go together. Such away-days are not uncommon. The venue is usually a diocesan pastoral centre or a religious house with an attractive ambience and accommodation adequate to absorb a group of anything from twenty to fifty or sixty people for seven or eight hours on end. The provision of meals need not present any problem: group members could be asked to take a packed lunch, with tea or coffee provided by the host community.

'An organised outing will take people away from their home environment for a few hours.'

The purpose of the away-day would obviously be partly social — people to get to know one another better — but it could also be educational. The programme could include items such as the following:

- Mid-morning, arrive at the centre either from the parish by coach or privately. Coffee on arrival.
- Morning session, lasting to lunch time. If children come they would have their own separate sessions organised and run by youth club leaders, sisters or sixth-form catechists. The session for the adults could take up the theme agreed on when the away-day was at the planning stage and opinions were sounded. This could be: (a) the latest Papal Letter; (b) the Year of . . .; (c) Baptism — how is it important? A special speaker would explore the topic with the adults, using modern techniques to involve the participants, breaking up the period into small and varied units. To be avoided at all costs is just talking, listening. Special effort should be made to make it enjoyable.
- After lunch, time for a chat and a stroll.
- Before tea, a film, film strip or slides, with plenty of opportunity to reflect, comment, question and discuss.
- After tea, communal preparation for the Eucharist. Choice of hymns, bidding, prayers, all in relation to the theme. If there are children, they should come together with the others for this preparation. Most groups will include some who can play an instrument: all this talent to be used. Even hymn practice has its social and educational value.

Of course the group organising the away-day could be quite different from a parish CWL or UCM. It could be just a particular group of parishioners; and the invitation could be extended to the entire parish in the hope that some hundreds of people with whole families, parents and children, could be persuaded to enrol.[1]

Alternatively, a parish away-day could be used to involve all interested parishioners in forward planning for the parish pastoral development.

NOTES

1. In a situation like this the parish of Southall, under Fr Michael Hollings, has experience of this type of parish away-day. St Mary's College, Strawberry Hill, was the venue. Quite a different programme would obviously be indicated here.

9: Pilgrimage

AS AN ACTIVITY of the Christian people, the pilgrimage is practically as old as Christianity itself. Nowadays, as a general rule, it takes one or other of two forms.

● There is the one-day pilgrimage to a local or national shrine — Aylesford, Walsingham, Coventry. The organisational procedure is very much the same as for the away-day. Coaches are engaged to transport groups of local people to the shrine. Everyone brings a packed lunch. Everyone is home by evening.

The local organising team should see to it that the pilgrims are given some briefing on the religious significance of the place they are to visit, and this is best done during the journey. The journey itself is of value: it is as much part of the pilgrimage as the actual visit to the shrine, a point which we might have learned from Chaucer and his Canterbury pilgrims. To ensure, therefore, that the journey is not just a gossip sandwiches and lemonade affair:

(i) ● The organisers should carefully plan a commentary to be spoken over the coach communication system by someone specially selected. This should give an account of the history and special significance of the shrine; noting the places the coach is passing through and arranging for it to stop at any spot of historical religious interest. Questions to the speaker should be encouraged. Appropriate prayers could be said, and hymns sung.

(ii ● On the return journey the pilgrims could be encouraged to share their impressions and religious experience. This 'share-in' could be conducted by a member of the organising team, preferably not the one who gave the outward journey talk. The coach microphone passed around would enable all to have the chance to contribute to, and to benefit from, this shared experience.

● There is also the pilgrimage to one of the traditional holy places involving air and/or sea travel and lasting for days and possibly weeks. For decades the national or diocesan pilgrimage to Lourdes has been, and still is, a feature of Catholic parish life. To this has now been added the pilgrimage to Rome, or to the Holy Land, with quite large groups making the long journeys. The travel agencies involved in organising these trips are well aware of the importance of ensuring that a religious educational commentary is provided at all stages of these journeys, without which there would be little to distinguish them from their non-religious counterparts. These longer pilgrimages, in particular those to the Holy Land, tend nowadays to be organised on an inter-faith basis, adding a welcome dimension to the experience. Perhaps in no other set of circumstances can one so easily and so sympathetically acquire an insight into the religious attitudes and life-vision of those of other religious traditions.

10: Residential weekend

MANY adult education projects involve attendance at meetings. Planning sessions, workshops, evening classes, study groups — all require the participants to meet at a specific place where the action takes place; and one of the tasks facing the organisers is to find a venue to suit the particular occasion. The parish hall, if there is one, can usually be adapted to the special requirements of most meetings of parishioners. Or it may be that the presbytery would be more suitable; or a room in somebody's home; or a classroom at the local evening institute; or an upstairs room in a pub. Occasionally the organisers might prefer to meet for a more than usually extended period of time, perhaps for a whole morning and afternoon, or for the entire day; and then it is much more difficult to find a suitable and available meeting place.

It has been partly to meet this situation that many English dioceses have in recent years established their own special pastoral centres. Specialist groups such as parish societies, school staffs and schoolchildren, and diocesan planning bodies, are making increasing use of the facilities offered by these centres. And as the centres are generally able to offer a certain amount of residential accommodation, a residential weekend course is now for the first time a genuine possibility. It probably has to be 'weekend' for the obvious reason that most people could never ordinarily make themselves free in mid-week.

There is a lot to be said in favour of the residential weekend as the venue for adult education. One very special advantage is, of course, the social dimension. People come not only for the talks, discussions and so on; they also meet socially, in groups or in pairs, in the canteen, in the common room, in their rooms, in the garden, on the lawn. And these rather casual and unplanned contacts often encourage a type of communication that would be impossible in the formal setting of a lecture or discussion group. The organisers of weekend study courses or conferences should make provision for these semi-formal exchanges by incorporating a reasonable amount of free time in their programme.

The organisers should ensure that their programme includes as wide a variety of activity as possible. The customary fare of talks plus discussion in groups should be spiced by the addition of simulation and role-play sessions, by the use of film or video tape, by setting up workshops to design or produce a musical, or a dramatic or a visual artistic illustration of the theme of the meeting. A Mass or morning or evening prayer session would normally be part of such a weekend meeting. This could with much profit be planned and conducted by people attending the weekend rather than the organisers.

HARO

11: *Marriage Encounter*

MARRIAGE Encounter[1], its supporters will tell you, is not an organisation: it is a movement. It is, however, one that has spread to more than fifty countries since it began some twenty years ago.

The goal which this worldwide movement sets before itself is the renewal of the Catholic Church through the sacrament of matrimony. The key to tapping the potential in this sacrament is communication between husband and wife. Good communication is only possible when husband and wife are willing to listen to each other, not just hearing words but actively listening. To achieve this, barriers have to be overcome — barriers that are built up, behaviour patterns adopted by husband and wife that allow them a comfortable conformity to relationship values proclaimed by our modern world.

To bring husband and wife together, Marriage Encounter[2] arranges residential weekends in diocesan pastoral centres, hotels or conference centres, in any convenient place. Twenty to twenty-five couples are the optimum number. The programme for the weekend consists of a series of presentations by three Catholic couples and a Catholic priest, all of whom are familiar with the Encounter procedure. During these presentations the couples and the priest talk of their personal experiences in their attempt to understand and live out the respective vocations of matrimony and holy orders. The couples then retire to their own rooms and discuss what they have heard.

For the couples attending, 'encounter' is a very personal and private experience. At no time are they expected to speak to the whole group. The accent of the weekend is on renewal, foremost the renewal of the couples' relationships and through this the renewal of family relationships and relationship to the Church.

As the weekend progresses, the couples are invited to explore as a sacrament their own experience of their relationship; to recognise that they did not just give the sacrament to one another on their wedding day, but that they continue to be that sacrament for one another every day in the way they love one another. This loving one another is the gift, the sign that they are to the rest of the Church. Starting from the simple gift of communication, the couple grow in the knowledge of who they are, and experience for themselves that they have a tremendous power in their lives for one another, a gift that is given for the building up of the Church.

Closely allied to Marriage Encounter is the Choice movement. Based on a residential weekend course for single adults aged from eighteen to thirty, Choice aims to facilitate the development of the individual as a Christian through a series of presentations on topics ranging from self knowledge through communication and sexuality to Christian vocation. The presenting team, which comprises a priest, a sister, a married couple and two single adults, stimulate group discussion and individual reflection by means of a series of talks rooted in their personal experiences.

The educational and supportive endeavour does not finish with the weekend. There are subsequent monthly meetings for discussion and liturgical celebration with the opportunity for mutual and sustained growth.

NOTES
1. This section has been contributed by David and Pauline Perkins.
2. Phone 01-992 5941.

12: Distance learning

THIS TERM, dear to professional educators in local authority evening institutes and to Open University tutors, covers a variety of activities, of which the chief in the present context are:

a) Correspondence courses

Several of these are advertised regularly in the press.[1] For a fee, one can enrol for a specific course in scripture or theology. A tutor is appointed who prescribes and supervises a programme of guided reading and written course work for each student. In some cases a brief week or ten-day residential vocation period is offered as part of the course.

b) Local Radio Programmes

Some local radio stations[1] have experimented with broadcasts of religious talks, coupled with an organised phone-in service available to listeners. The speaker receives a certain number of queries or comments from house groups meeting in the area whose members have listened to this talk. He/she replies or gives comments to all the listeners.

The much more widely publicised and much greater success of the Open University televised programmes indicates the tremendous untapped possibilities which the new media can offer to the development of Distance Learning.

NOTES
1. e.g. Religious studies, O level courses, Kilburn Polytechnic, Neasden Centre, Light/Life. (Neasden Grail course)
2. e.g. Radio Medway, 1979-80

13: Religious literature

THE PUBLICATIONS of the Catholic Truth Society, the weekly issues of the Catholic press, and the theological, scriptural and religious writings of Catholic and non-Catholic authors in a number of religious journals and publications, have up to now been for all intents and purposes the only means available to Catholic adults wishing to advance their own religious education. Some parishes make special provision for this limited but very important section of the community. The CTS box is kept well stocked. A large parish might even have its own bookshop. Parishioners are regularly exhorted to take a weekly Catholic newspaper; to subscribe to one or more religious periodicals.

The quality and range of the literature thus provided can vary enormously. Lives of well known religious personalities are always popular. There will always be a demand for simple theological and apologetic presentations of the elements of Catholic belief and practice. Liturgical manuals, including missals and the Prayer of the Church, are increasingly in demand. Sometimes, very occasionally, the writings of contemporary theologians and scripture scholars, and increasingly the Bible itself, are included; and an ever growing number of Catholics who know about these read them.

Never — well, hardly ever — does one find books or booklets on group activities and group dynamics, communication skills, studies of pastoral strategy, the literature that attempts to answer the query of the dedicated post-Vatican II Catholic: how can I become a more effective Christian in my life? And there is a growing demand for these.

14: New ministries

THE APPEARANCE of new lay ministries is a significant feature of post-Vatican II Catholicism. It may be of increasing importance in the years to come — provided, that is, that the laity will be induced through this means to offer their services to the Church. But they will be slow to come forward unless some specialist tuition and training in content and skills is provided. How can this be done?

● The extraordinary *minister of the Eucharist* is the first we should consider. It is now quite commonplace in our churches to see Holy Communion distributed by lay people in addition to the parish clergy and religious. The ministry is, however, one which would appeal to a number of parishioners if a training programme were provided for prospective candidates. Such a programme would include:

☐ Theology: what the Eucharist is; its part in the divine plan.
☐ History: how the Eucharist has been distributed to the faithful at various epochs in the Church's story; in particular the way it was administered in the early Church.
☐ The regulations governing the ministry of Holy Communion, e.g., what to do if the host is dropped, if the consecrated wine is spilled, and so on.

● *The reader.* It might seem on the face of it that the only qualification one should look for in a reader — i.e. one who is asked to read one or other of the first two readings from the lectionary at Sunday Mass — is that he/she should have a good voice and should know how to announce the message audibly and intelligently. If, however, one regards the reader as someone specially selected and commissioned for the task, then one would expect that he/she would have some sort of awareness of the office that was being discharged: would realise, for example, that, as Vatican II has stated, one of the four ways in which Christ is really present to the congregation attending Mass is through 'the promulgation of the Word'. The reader has, therefore, a very important ministerial role in presenting the readings: he/she is the one who makes Christ present in the promulgation of the Good News.

A training programme for readers should, then, include:

☐ A study of the scriptures — old Testament, Pauline Epistles, the four Gospels — to give the reader a sense of the significance of the Message he/she is called to announce.

☐ Some elementary schooling in elocution, which in no way suppresses regional accents.

● *The parish communications officer.* It has more than once been suggested that a vitally necessary parish official is a communications officer. His/her function would be:

☐ To receive direct the diocesan information sheets and *Ad Clerum,* and filter the relevant information to the parish organisations concerned.

☐ To receive direct the publication *Briefings,* which contains documents and official news releases from Catholic Information Services; to read them and pass them in full or in summary to the appropriate parish officers, organisations, societies and the editor of the parish newsletter.

☐ To attend lay or lay/clergy deanery meetings.

☐ To receive direct notification of the activities of the diocesan education and special welfare agencies.

A training course for such officials would include:

☐ Communication skills appropriate to the duties of parish communications officer.

15: Parent preparation for the sacraments

PARENTS should of course be involved in what school and parish do to prepare their children for first confession and Communion. They should be informed of the process and invited to co-operate.[1] This is not, however, what is intended here. The aim of 'parent preparation' courses is to help parents clarify what their Christianity means to them, so as to enable their children to glimpse what is the inner dynamism which energises their parents' religious practice. This is what parents — whether they wish to do so or not, whether they are conscious of the process or not — communicate to their children.

Preparation for baptism

It is quite remarkable, when one reflects on it, that so much energy, so much fuss, emotion, heat and aggro has centred on the first reception of the Sacraments of the Eucharist and Penance, while the Sacrament of Baptism passes, or is by-passed, quietly in an hour or less on a Sunday afternoon.

It should not be beyond the bounds of possibility to involve parents from the beginning, i.e. from the pregnancy of the first child, in preparing for the first sacrament the child is to receive. The benefits would be twofold. In the first place the parents would get a richer insight into life, into Christianity, into their own vocation as Christians. They would also be enabled to see their role as educators in the home from the very beginning; and the subsequent transition to school would not seem to be, as it often does, a handing over of responsibility, but the entering into a further partnership — the next stage in the lifelong religious education of their child.

How can this parent preparation be done? The parish priest regularly receives advance notice of requests for baptism, so that it should be possible to form a group of three or four couples who are expecting a child at near enough the same time. The preparation could be as little as three or four sessions held in the homes of one of the couples. The content might be something like this:

☐ The gift of life. What is life going to mean for my child? Hopes and fears. Thanksgiving ceremony.
☐ What does baptism do? What is original sin?
☐ The role of parents as Christian educators.
☐ Study of the New Rite of Infant Baptism — Symbolism, Sacrament.

The ideal people to give these sessions to the parents are other parents. They would, of course, need a certain amount of training in theology, communication skills, basic psychology and sociology, and in the revised liturgy of infant baptism.

Preparation for Penance

So much paper, so much anxiety, so much debate on the time appropriate for first reception of the Sacrament of Reconciliation! At last we seem to be moving into a saner mood where chronology retires in favour of the principle of readiness. And the sacrament is seen less as prerequisite to the Eucharist than as basic to any Christian in his ongoing journey through life. With this growing understanding the parental role becomes at once clearer and more important.

From the first stirrings of the new baby in search of basic needs, the education for penance and reconciliation/conversion of heart can begin. It is a necessary follow-up to infant baptism. With the parents more or less clear that baptism is initiation into the baptism with which Jesus longed to be baptised, namely his death for us on the cross, the programme of preparation for 'penance' is seen as long-term. It is a continuous orientation of the infant into a life where the centre of attention gradually shifts from self to others. The awakening consciousness of the child can coincide with a sensitivity to the presence of and the needs of others, first in the immediate family and then on into the wider world of relatives, friends and others. Given an awareness of the psychological development of a child, the parents can foster attitudes of unselfishness and generosity, giving praise for efforts made and encouraging sorrow for failures, and all in the light of a loving God who like the parents has the opinion that all in all 'Mary is a good girl' or 'John is a good boy'. Given this foundation, supported and reinforced in the school, the child will be into the way of conversion, of penance, of reconciliation, by the time that he/she can distinguish God our Father from Mummy, Daddy and other significant adults. The preparation is already done, the conscience is already sensitive. The visit to the priest in 'confession' is but a continuation of a process already begun at home in the post-baptismal period. The child's first confession is a significant stage in a journey already well on the way. It is not just something connected with going to church and receiving sacraments.

The preparation course might again take the form of three or four talks/discussions in the parish or school hall. The topics could include:

□ Our idea of God: Lawgiver? Judge? Loving Father?
□ Sin — what it really is.
□ Conscience: 'How do I know I am right?'
□ The New Rite of the Sacrament of Reconciliation.

Preparation for first Holy Communion

Young children are less likely to get a wrong initial attitude to Holy Communion than to confession. In their simple way they readily accept that Holy Communion is a personal encounter with Christ who gives Himself to them in the form of bread. A preparation course for parents might therefore attempt to give *them* some insights that their children could never, at their present stage, be capable of. It could include the following:

□ The scriptural account of the promise of the Eucharist (John VI) and the Last Supper.
□ The history of the Church's practice in regard to the Eucharist.
□ The 'Real Presence' of Christ in the Eucharist.
□ The Mass as the daily renewal of our Baptism.

Preparation for the Sacrament of Confirmation

This can be for someone baptised in infancy the means of celebrating a personal decision to become a Christian in spirit and in truth. What is the parents' role? Assuming this decision to be freely made, the parents would need help and the co-operation of other parents to appreciate the problems, the struggles, the difficulties, the pressures on the emerging adult. Their role is one of example, support, encouragement, listening and standing back, while at the same time making their own stance crystal clear on moral issues, especially those which touch social life, justice, injustice, politics. The young should not be appealed to on grounds of obedience and loyalty: they should rather be assisted and encouraged to be positively critical of all around them, including religion and religious structures. Only in such a climate can the youngsters feel free to assess and choose. A parents' preparation course should therefore include:

☐ The psychology of the adolescent.
☐ Who is Christ? What the Scripture tells us about Him.
☐ The Church that Christ founded.
☐ Freedom and authority: how to reconcile?
☐ What it means to be a Christian in today's world.

NOTES

1. In many parishes in recent years, whether there is a parish school or not, the method of preparation for the sacraments associated with the names of Christianne Brusselmans or Wim Saris is followed, a special feature of which is the intimate involvement of the parents in the preparation programme.

16: Communication skills

THERE are many passages in Scripture which one could quote in support of the truth that God communicates directly with man: 'Speak, Lord, thy servant heareth . . .'; 'and there I shall speak to her heart'. All prayer of petition is grounded on this assumption. However, the ordinary way in which the word of God comes to people is through other people. 'He who hears you hears me,' said Our Lord. It was for his disciples to mediate the Good News to the world.

In our age we are conscious as never before of the tremendous importance of good communication. Techniques and skills of transmission and reception are being constantly improved and refined. The medium is the message! The Christian Church ignores this brutal truth at its peril. In fact there are many indications that the Church is well aware of the importance of communication skills and techniques in the transmission of religious truths. The Church, however, has been very slow to do anything about it, yet at the same time is calling on the laity to play a more active part in communicating the Good News to the world.

In parish and deanery and diocese, the laity are being enrolled in impressive numbers to swell the apostolate. Parishes are instructed to set up parish councils. Planning groups are formed to inaugurate religious study courses and discussion programmes. Parish and diocesan representatives are commissioned to advise on the multiple ways in which the truths of faith can be transmitted by parents and teachers to the young, by adults to adults, by believers to non-believers. New ministries are to be established. All the resources of the media are to be used in this great modern missionary thrust. All this implies training.

How does one function, to take one example, as an active member of a group, be that group a pastoral planning committee, or an adult discussion group, or the parish council itself? Most people have heard, vaguely, of 'group dynamics' and are worried by it. But if they have not made a study of it they are helpless in the face of the 'dominant member' who hogs the discussion so that nobody can speak. There is a simple technique to be adopted to deal with this if it happens; but if the chairman hasn't heard of it, then the group disintegrates in sheer frustrated inability to cope with this common and simple occurrence.

How many people are aware that there is an art of listening, which is as important as, if not more important than, the art of speaking?

Hidden in our congregations are Catholics professionally qualified in the field of communication skills, business organisation, management consultancy, radio and television. The time has come when they should be invited to put their experience and expertise at the service of the Church.

A course in communication skills for lay people, priests, religious who might wish to improve their ability to communicate in everyday life and in their work for the Church might include the following:

— basic skills of communication: person to person;
— the art of listening;

— serving in a committee;
— speaking;
— group participation;
— handling the discussion;
— the art of persuasion; and
— written communication, memos, newsletters.

17: Training the leaders

'THE SON of Man has come not to have service done to him but to serve . . .' This quote from the sayings of the founder of Christianity is surely the key to all the heart-searching in the modern Church for a substitute for the word Leader. The many attempts to rid ourselves of the overtones of dominance and superiority which the word carries, by using such alternatives as 'animator', 'activator', 'enabler', 'facilitator', have not solved the problem. Everywhere there is a desire to evade the authority position. Yet the exercise of authority is essential for the working of every human institution, from the family to the state.

In Christ we see the divine authority incarnated — 'all authority in heaven and earth is given to me'. Yet it was exercised for service: 'I am here as one who serves'. His whole life shows what is meant by service.

So let us do two things quickly. Let us bring back without any shame or apology the concept of authority, in family, in school, in parish. But let that authority be clearly seen to be linked incontrovertibly to the ministry of service. All this is by way of preface to this section, which is concerned with those whose function it is to train others for particular duties of service in the Church. This is the age of decentralisation, of power-sharing, of collegiality, of the establishment of new ministries, of new forms of service. A new importance is seen in the local community, and a new significance in the initiatives that arise there. The local community is encouraged to provide itself with its own officers, its own leadership. Leaders are not just born: the skills of leadership can be learned.

All this implies training. Presuming that the local leaders are there for the discovering, they would still require a modicum of training before they should be asked to assume these new roles. In the world of business and industry, in the civil service, in local government, the people are well aware of the vital importance of training. Courses in business management, in organisational skills, in industrial psychology, are regularly prescribed for top executives and middle management. Initial crash courses are regularly followed up by in-service courses.

The Church has not been unaware of the evolution within her own structure. And in this context the Church realises there is a lot to learn. There are four areas of knowledge and skills in which those engaged in adult religious education ought to be experienced and qualified, and therefore trained:

— *Communication skills.* A working knowledge of these skills (cf. preceding section) is necessary for every worker in the field of adult education.
— *Religious studies.* Equally necessary is a sufficient knowledge of the Church's doctrinal and moral teaching, of the Old and New Testament, of Church history, of liturgy and Christian spirituality.
— *Leadership skills.* Those who accept a position of leadership need to be prepared for all the eventualities that may arise.
— *Adult education,* its theory and practice.

In effect all this would necessitate a variety of training sessions, dependent on the function the trainee is being prepared to operate. In particular:

□ *Discussion group leaders* need training in the theology, i.e. the 'content', of the topic under discussion, and in the communication skills, techniques and procedures of group discussion. In the training course these could be interwoven in such a way that the prospective leaders learn the one in the context of the other. To select and employ leaders on the basis of their qualities of leadership alone, without such a course, would be unfair both to the leaders themselves and to the groups they join. The training course should include such skills as:

— how to form a group; how to promote its adhesiveness and contain its disruptiveness;

— how to give group members confidence and reassurance, guaranteeing that differences can be discussed and feelings revealed in safety;
— how to know when to intervene to protect an individual or the group as a whole;
— how to relate to other members of the group, especially problem members, cordially, self-critically, and not too earnestly;
— how to resolve a situation of conflict; and
— how to encourage the organic growth and development of the group.

□ *Parish and area representatives,* i.e. those with special responsibility to advise on adult religious educational projects and activities, and to liaise with the diocesan centre, should be given a more thorough course in communication skills and in religious studies. They are just the sort who would appreciate that knowledge of only one area of the Church's belief and teaching would be inadequate for their task. Opportunity should therefore be provided to them to deepen and to develop their understanding of their faith in a variety of ways.

□ *Course tutors,* i.e. those who organise and conduct series of talks, lectures, study courses, discussion group programmes at parish, deanery or area level, need very special training. Their particular task includes, first, being fully aware of the immediate local situation, the kind of people who may attend, their hopes and expectations, their fears. Second, they need to be able to exercise authority so that people feel secure and confident that things will go well, that timing is adhered to, that practical arrangements will be made, that the course will be geared at all times to meet the needs of the generality of the participants. Third, they need humour and good sense to create a good social atmosphere, so that people will not only benefit from hearing the speaker but will enjoy themselves and relate to each other. Lastly, they should realise that they are the continuity element in the course, linking together the contributions made by various speakers, providing summaries, ensuring and conducting evaluation at the end, and laying the foundation for follow-on.

It is not an easy matter to be a good course tutor; and regrettably the suitability and qualifications for the role are often, wrongly, taken for granted. It is for the diocese to provide proper training and guidance for these key people.

18: Ministry to the housebound

IN ANY diocesan programme of adult religious education, the housebound would probably figure well down the list of priorities. Two categories of people make up the housebound: the very elderly and the physically handicapped; and each group can have the further disadvantage of being in hospital. Yet each of these groups deserves the special care of the Christian community.

The housebound elderly are also a diverse group of people, and it would be a mistake if they were all treated in the same way. At one extreme are the men and women of solid faith, some of whom were perhaps leaders of the community a decade ago, whose religion is now, in the twilight of their days, their mainstay and their strength. These ask nothing more than that they be kept in touch. At the other extreme are those who may have attended the religious functions of the parish all their lives but who now, without those props, experience a genuine loss of faith. The final consequence could be an inner despair.

The handicapped are again a diverse group; but among them could be some who, though bedridden and therefore unable to attend parish functions, are still mentally alert, anxious not to be written off by the community of which they are nominally members, and capable of a rich spiritual and intellectual life if given the opportunity.

If the parish is to do anything for any of these people, then, as they cannot attend a function in common with others, someone must go to visit them where they are, in their homes or in a hospital ward. Here are some ways in which the ministry to the housebound might operate:

□ On the occasion of parish feasts, e.g. Christmas, Easter, and special celebrations such as a visit from the bishop, an ordination, a mission, it should be possible to arrange for those who are not totally immobile to be brought to the parish church. This would require special transport, help with wheelchairs, special facilities. The young people of the parish are usually ready and willing to undertake this; but, as most experienced folk realise, their good will must be harnessed and organised in some way for effective and sustained action.[1]

□ A recent development, *tapes for the elderly,* are now being produced by the Catholic publishing houses,[2] and are on sale in the bookshops. These tapes offer a series of recordings of readings, homilies, music, etc, appropriate to the liturgical seasons or to special events such as a papal visit. The elderly housebound can of course acquire these tapes and play them to themselves, and it is partly the intention of the publishers that they should be used in this way. Another way to use this material, however, would be for a parish group, preferably of young adults, to offer to pay visits alone or in pairs to the old people, with the proviso made above that some organisation and even training would be necessary. During the course of the visit they could listen to part or the whole of the tape together and then chat about it, making sure that the visitor assumed more and more the role of listener in the conversation.

□ Many parishes are beginning to use their groups of *special ministers of the Eucharist* to bring Holy Communion to the housebound. Here is a one-to-one relationship already established. It could be possible to develop this into a genuine adult religious education activity by arranging for the minister on a limited number of occasions to extend the visit in order to discuss a topic or a series of topics — a kind of para-liturgy with dialogue homily — with the housebound person.

□ Lastly, as the members of the parish are often quite unaware of the existence of the housebound in their midst, so from time to time the Sunday liturgy could include as homily material the topic of the handicapped and elderly. Many of Our Lord's miracles which occur in the Sunday readings lend themselves to such treatment, and His concern for these people is crystal clear from the Gospels. Somebody from the diocesan agency for the handicapped[3] could be invited as special preacher on some of these occasions. The same agency could be asked to give a mini training course to those in the parish who wish to help in this field. A talk on the subject could also be included from time to time in the parish religious education programme.

NOTES

1. This was done very successfully at Holy Road Parish, Watford, on the occasion of a renewal week.
2. e.g. *The Sower,* January 1983: Sister Deirdre Ford's article on tapes for the elderly, published by Mayhew McCrimmon Ltd.
3. In Westminster, St Joseph's Centre, Hendon, NW4.

19: Ministry to prisoners

THE LEAST practised of the corporal works of mercy must surely be 'to visit the imprisoned'. In defence of the many good Christians who might have been willing to implement this injunction of the Founder, it should be said that the authorities of HM Prisons do not make this an easy thing to do. Visits to prisoners are governed by strict regulations. While this is true, there are still possibilities of access to prisoners within the system.

What sort of activity would prison inmates wish to attend? Anything that would get them out of their cells for an hour or two would provide an attraction. Motivation for any educational activity is only secondary to the prime desire to be free. So the question is rather which among all the options would get a high rating, granted the chief interest is in being out and about. Experience has shown that any moralising that tends to 'get at' the prisoners is a waste of time. The wall of resistance renders it useless. However, Scripture, Old and New Testament, prove acceptable, as the content is from the book, is objective, and on the face of it not aimed specifically at them.

'During chaplain's hour, prisoners can meet their chaplain and talk to him on any subject he cares to raise.'

They can, so to speak, take the message or leave it. They can reject the inherent appeal of the Word or internalise and accept it. (Interestingly, it is at that personal level of their inner lives that the prisoners are in fact still free.) Church history, doctrine, spirituality and even prayer, are acceptable for the same reasons, particularly if they are treated ecumenically in the broadest sense of that word.

The speakers on the course should be sensible, matter-of-fact men and women. If it is possible to use auxiliaries, i.e. demonstrators, as discussion group leaders, then these should be interesting, exciting, attractive, not predictable and conventional people.

An alternative to educational time is to use the 'chaplain's hour' when the prisoners are entitled to meet their chaplain and talk with him on any subject he cares to raise. This is an informal, unstructured meeting, ideal for a genuine exchange of views. It has been used variously and with different degrees of success.[1]

NOTES

1. An interesting experiment along these lines has been initiated by the chaplains of HM Prison Wormwood Scrubbs with assistance from the WAREC team and the Westminster Missionaries.

20: Catechumenate

THIS has been defined[1] as 'a training period for the whole Christian life'. In the early Church the catechumenate was the initiation period for converts to the Christian faith. It lasted anything from one to seven years. In modern times it has often been suggested that the Church should revive the Catechumenate in some form. The Vatican Council eventually decreed its 'restoration, revision, and accommodation to local traditions'.[2] In many missionary areas it is already established.

In 1972 the Sacred Congregation for Divine Worhsip promulgated an important document, *The Rite of the Christian Initiation of Adults*. This in effect decreed the reintroduction of the catechumenate in four specific stages, each with its corresponding rites. The four stages are:

☐ The pre-catechumenate, a time for hearing the first preaching of the Gospel.

☐ The catechumenate proper, the period set aside for a complete catechesis.

☐ The period of purification and enlightenment, of illumination (usually in Lent) for a more profound spiritual preparation. This period ends with the Baptism of the catechumen.

☐ The post-baptismal catechesis, the so-called *mystogogia* (Easter season), the period in which the newly baptised have experience of the sacraments and the Christian community.[3]

All this implies in each of the four stages a great deal of adult religious education. At the Liverpool Congress, 1980, it was even suggested[4] that the RCIA might provide the framework for the whole of adult religious education for the future.

It is probably too soon to anticipate the effect which this document and the organisation it recommends will have on activities already existing in the field of adult education and formation. The Roman authors of the preface to the RCIA recommend again and again the utmost flexibility in adapting the process to local needs and traditions.

In implementing its recommendations, we can, however, see a new area of adult religious education opening up. But there are difficulties, as a modern American author, who has been among the first to attempt an assessment of the pastoral implications of the new document, has been quick to point out. He notes that[5] 'the RCIA is primarily for new Catholic Christians ... but to dump five catechumens into a group of thirty Catholics who want to update themselves is to mix apples and oranges. The catechumens can get lost ... However, since the same process of deepening conversion holds for new and old Catholics, we hope it will spread into general parish renewal'.

The term catechumenate has been adopted by many other movements in the modern Church. Worthy of special note in this context is 'The New Catechumenate', of Spanish and Italian origin, which like the RCIA has conversion of heart as central to its aim.

The focus is on Word, Eucharist and community. The catechesis on the Word is of the simplest in its exposition, and so is accessible to people at all educational levels. The weekly Eucharist is celebrated in a place other than the parish church, and always on a Saturday evening. The community is the name given to each group that undergoes an initial catechesis. The commitment of each community is to two weekly meetings, including the Eucharist, one full day a month, and a weekend several times a year with the other communities of the parish or neighbouring parishes. Long term, the hope is that the good effects of this deep personal conversion and dedication of this relatively small number of people will spread into the whole parish.

NOTES

1. *Ad Gentes,* par 14.
2. RCIA, par 2.
3. RCIA, par 7d.
4. *Easter People,* par 148.
5. *New Wine, Old Wineskins,* James Dunning (Sadlier, 1981), p25.

Postscript

IN THEIR first book,[1] Father Kevin and Sister Gemma expressed the considered opinion that the work of directing diocesan agencies for adult religious education should be in the hands of lay people. In 1981 they put their theory into practice and stepped aside from leading the work they had pioneered. It is my privilege to continue the work in their tradition and with their help.

The climate in which we work is a changed one. On the one side, the repercussions from the National Pastoral Congress (1980) and the visit of Pope John Paul II (1982): on the other, a decline in traditional patterns of Catholic practice. Slowly and sometimes painfully the people are growing in confidence to apply their critical faculties to their religious belief and practice. The Church must respond in practical terms to this aspiration towards healthy growth.

To meet these needs we need educators trained in all that is best in adult education, theory and practice, and able to benefit from the openings for adult learning both inside the Church organisation and outside in the local authority education system. Such training will need funding.

It will take time before the work of adult religious education is properly staffed throughout the country: all the more important, then, that efforts be co-ordinated and good ideas pooled. Working with fellow Christians in the common mission is not an optional extra, particularly at this level: practical schemes must be found for this co-operation. Again, we have a unique experience to offer other countries, and also much to learn from them. Our mission is to all nations, and must not be confined.

Adult religious education cannot be limited to any one way, or even any twenty ways. Content and method must be continually adapted to changing needs and circumstances. Mistakes are permitted — provided that we learn from them!

Our most recent experiment is 'Theology for Parishioners', an attempt to create a coherent and cohesive programme for adults which takes seriously the theory that adult religious education is a lifetime's work. It combines many elements of the twenty ways outlined in the book and presents new challenges. It is exciting in that it combines the skills of specialist theologians and communications technicians in the Church. It is challenging in that it puts the learning firmly in the context of the local situation. It seems to be meeting the need felt by adults of all ages and backgrounds for better understanding of their faith and greater expertise in communicating this understanding to others.

We Christians, and especially we Catholic Christians, have strong theory and enormous potential: if we dare put it into practice, it would release a Good News revolution in our land.

Tony McCaffry

NOTES

1.

Into the Future, Mayhew McCrimmon Ltd, 1977.